Hsüan-hua

THE WONDERFUL DHARMA

LOTUS FLOWER

SUTRA.

TRANSLATED INTO CHINESE BY TRIPITAKA MASTER KUMARAJIVA
OF YAO CH'IN

volume one: introduction

with the commentary of

Tripitaka Master Hua

Translated into English by
THE BUDDHIST TEXT TRANSLATION SOCIETY
SAN FRANCISCO
1977

Translated by the Buddhist Text Translation
Society

Primary translation: Bhikshuni Heng Yin
Reviewed by: Bhikshuni Heng Ch'ih
Edited by: Upasika Kuo-lin Lethcoe
Certified by: The Venerable Master Hua

For information address:

    Sino American Buddhist Association
    Gold Mountain Monastery
    1731 15th Street
    San Francisco, California 94103
    U.S.A.
    (415) 621-5202
    (415) 861-9672

LC 77-87782
ISBN 0-917512-16-2

CONTENTS

Shakyamuni Buddha

Tripitaka Master Hsüan Hua

TRANSLATOR'S INTRODUCTION

Shakyamuni Buddha appeared in the world, we are told in *The Lotus Sutra,* because of the causes and conditions of the one great question. And what is the one great question? It is the question of the birth and death of all living beings. In this volume, the Buddhist Text Translation Society presents in translation the Venerable Master Hua's introduction to *The Lotus Sutra,* the Sutra proper, with commentary, to follow in coming volumes.

The world is beset with problems. We hear of them constantly. There are problems in the home, in our schools, problems with the ecology, and problems with the local, state, and national government, extending to problems in world-relations. Yet, all of these problems can be traced back to the one great problem: the problem of birth and death. In other words, where did we come from? Where are we going?

In *The Lotus Sutra,* the final, highest teaching of the Buddha, we are given the answer to that question, or rather given the means, the tools, with which we may, through our own diligent cultivation, discover that answer within ourselves by realizing our own, inherent Buddha-nature. In his commentary to this Sutra, the Venerable Master Hua brings the Lotus teachings fully to life with many lively stories, anecdotes, and analogies. He presents the Buddha's teachings in such a way that their application to us, in the present age, is immediately obvious. He urges his students to take the Buddhadharma as it was originally intended and to practice what they learn. By putting what we know into practice we can realize the Buddha within our own minds. But to merely understand, and mouth the words, is utterly useless:

> You may speak of it wonderfully,
>   speak of it well,
> But if you don't walk down it,
>   it's not the Way.

Walking the Way can be summed up in the three-fold study of morality, samadhi, and wisdom. Today we find a proliferation of pseudo-Good Knowing Advisors who ignore the Buddha's moral precepts, the very foundation upon which cultivation rests. They lead themselves and their followers to a dangerous pass:

> Confused teachers, teaching confusion,
> So that with one teaching, two misunderstand.
> The teacher plummets to the hells;
> The disciples follow with their hats in hand.

The Venerable Master Hua, Chairperson of the Sino-American Buddhist Association, Abbot of Gold Mountain Monastery and Dean of the International Institute for the Translation of Buddhists Texts, is a genuine Good Knowing Advisor. He has come to the West to transmit the Orthodox Teaching of Shakyamuni Buddha. Over the past ten years he has expounded daily upon the major Great Vehicle Sutras. On June 17, 1968, at the Buddhist Lecture Hall in San Francisco, the Master began lecturing on *The Surangama Sutra* to a group of forty students during a ninety-six day Sutra Study and Meditation Session. Each lecture took a minimum of two hours to deliver and translate. When it became obvious that the Sutra was too long to finish on schedule, the Master increased his lecturing from twice to three times a day, adding a lecture in the mornings as well as in the afternoons and evenings. Finally, by the end of the Summer, he was lecturing four times a day!

When the Session was over, many of the students took up permanent residence in San Francisco, moving from Seattle, and sacrificing many academic credits in the process. A large gathering of disciples were present on November 10, 1968 when the Master began lecturing on *The Wonderful Dharma Lotus Flower Sutra*. The Master lectured daily on that Sutra, twice daily on weekends, until two years, and over three hundred and fifty lectures, later, on November 10, 1970, the assembly was concluded.

The Wonderful Dharma Lotus Flower Sutra was delivered by the Buddha near the end of his teaching career to reveal the Real Dharma, the miraclous Dharma; all previous teachings are considered to be provisional-- used to lead his disciples to the level where they might understand the doctrine of universal salvation contained in the Lotus teaching. For this reason, this is a most important Sutra, and a clear understanding of it is necessary for all who wish to truly understand the Buddha-dharma.

To return to the one great question: The Venerable Master has said, "Human life is a round-trip affair.

When you leave you will always return. If you understand how you were born you will understand the problem of death." But that understanding comes only through study and practice of the Buddhadharma.

We have many problems, yes, but we have much to be grateful for. The Buddha has shown us the way to liberation. Our teacher, the Venerable Master Hua, has brought the Buddha's teaching, orthodox and entire, to the West, so that we may understand it and practice it. In his great wisdom and great compassion he tirelessly expounds upon the principles and brings them to life for us now.

We present this volume as a clear guide. It is up to each one of us, however, to follow it and quickly attain to Buddhahood. Thus, solving the problem of birth and death, we can return to help all living beings to do the same. In this way, we can, in some small measure, repay the kindness of the Buddhas, Bodhisattvas, and our teacher, Master Hua.

Bhikshuni Heng-yin
International Institute for the
Translation of Buddhist Texts
San Francisco, May 3, 1977

Editor's Preface

   Traditionally, Buddhists regard *The Lotus Sutra* as one of the Buddha's last sermons containing his final revelation on the universality of salvation, the true nature of Buddhahood, and the best and universally applicable means of attaining Buddhahoood; above all, it vigorously advances the position that the superior person not only knows the way to ultimate bliss and knowledge, but also helps others to find the way. It is appropriate therefore, that the great modern Chinese missionary, the Venerable Master Hua, should choose to lecture on this Sutra to his American disciples.
   Dharma Master Hua stands firmly in the tradition of erudite and practicing Buddhist teachers and missionaries. His commentary provides much doctrinal information for those interested in the history of religions or in modern Buddhist theory. Scholars will find, for example, that although he uses the *T'ien-t'ai* system of classification, he has not feared to depart from tradition by bringing his own insight to bear on the principles behind the categories. He sees *The Lotus Sutra* as containing the Buddha's purest and most complete Teaching. All other Sutras constitute ways in which the most perfect teacher, the Buddha, out of compassion for less endowed beings, broke down his ultimate doctrine into readily understandable steps whereby students received the necessary preparation for understanding and believing *The Lotus Sutra's* teachings.
   Ultimately, the Venerable Master Hua's commentary will prove most invaluable to those who not only study Buddhist doctrines, but also seek the translate Buddhist theory into practice. Since these lectures were delivered to the newly founded American Sangha, their purpose purpose was to provide the principles for right action leading to ultimate Buddhahood. Frequently, the Master's illustrations aptly indicate a new way of looking at

the world around us or describe a specific attitudinal change to purify our conduct. In this way, he shows the applications of *The Lotus Sutra's* teachings, which predate the Christian era, to the problems of all living beings in our complexly related age. Herein lies the implementation of the Bodhisattva ideal--the hope that we may all work diligently together and for each other to realize our inherent Buddhanatures.

Upasika Kuo-lin Lethcoe, Ph.D.

PART I.

The Five Periods & the Eight Teachings

In explaining Sutras, some use the methods of the *T'ien T'ai* School and some use those of the *Hsien Shou* School, two great teaching schools of Chinese Buddhism. The *T'ien T'ai* School was systematized by the Great Master *Chih-che (Chih-i,* A.D. 538-597) who divided the Buddha's Sutras into Five Periods and Eight Teachings. The Five Periods are:

1. The Avatamsaka Period,
2. the Agama Period,
3. the Vaipulya Period,
4. the Prajna Period, and
5. the Dharma Flower and Mahaparinirvana Periods.

Within the Five Periods, Eight Teachings are distinguished:

1. The Storehouse Teaching,
2. the Pervasive Teaching,
3. the Separate Teaching,
4. the Perfect Teaching,
5. the Sudden Teaching,
6. the Gradual Teaching,
7. the Secret Teaching, and

8. the Unfixed Teaching.

Each of the Five Periods listed above is likened to five kinds of milk products as will be seen.

1. The Avatamsaka Period. After his enlightenment, the Buddha first spoke the *Avatamsaka Sutra*. The Sutra consists of three volumes, only the last of which exists in the human realm, the other two being stored in the Dragon Palace.

Having mastered all the literature in the world, the Bodhisattva Dragon Tree *(Nagarjuna)* went to the Dragon Palace to read the Tripitaka. While there, he memorized the last volume of the *Avatamsaka Sutra*. Since he had the ability to memorize anything after it had passed his eyes only once, he read the Sutra once and brought the last volume back with him in his memory.

The Buddha spoke the *Avatamsaka Sutra* for twenty-one days, but only the Bodhisattvas heard it. Those Arhats and Bhikshus of the Small Vehicle did not even see him. It is said,

> They had eyes, but did not see
>   the Reward-body of the Buddha;
> They had ears, but did not hear
>   the Perfect-Sudden Teaching.

They failed to see the ten-thousand foot tall Reward-body which the Buddha manifested. We may think that ten-thousand feet is very tall, but compared to Amitabha Buddha's Reward-body, it is very small. As the verse in praise of Amitabha Buddha says,

> The fine light from between his brows
>   shines as high as five Mount Sumerus;
> His purple eyes are clear and broad
>   as four great seas.

Most people are unable to imagine the size of one great sea, let alone four. The enlightened patriarchs of the past, who saw Amitabha Buddha's fine marks and adornments, wrote such a verse in his praise. Compared to Amitabha Buddha's fine light and violet eyes, everything else is very small, including the ten-thousand foot Reward-body which Shakyamuni Buddha manifested. But those of the Two Vehicles, the Sound Hearers *(Shravakas)* and Condition-enlightened Ones *(Pratyeka Buddhas)*, did not see it, even though they had eyes. They had ears, but they didn't hear the Perfect-Sudden Teaching. Those of the Two Vehicles had ears, but they did not hear the Buddha speak the *Avatamsaka Sutra's* great Dharma. So the period of speaking the *Avatamsaka Sutra* was for teaching great Bodhisattvas, the Mahasattvas of the ten directions.

The Five Periods of the Buddha's teaching are represented by an analogy to milk products and to the rising sun. The Avatamsaka Period is compared to whole milk, raw and unprocessed. It is also likened to the newly risen sun which first shines on the high peaks. The Dharma spoken by the Buddha is analogous to the sun and the high peaks are analogous to the Bodhisattvas to whom the Buddha first spoke the Dharma. They are like the high peaks because, among living beings, the Bodhisattvas are the highest.

2. The Agama Period. Agama, a Sanskrit word, means "incomparable Dharma," for none of the dharmas of non-Buddhist religions can compare with it; it surpasses all of them. During this period the Small Vehicle Teaching was set forth. It can be compared to coagulated milk which is extracted from whole milk and which is easy for children to digest. Straight, raw milk is very strong and nourishing and so it is used to represent the Avatamsaka Teaching.

The Agama Teaching is like coagulated milk, good for children. When the Buddha taught the Agamas the sun had risen a hundred feet and its light reached the dark places in the valleys where the light of the newly risen sun of the Avatamsaka did not reach, so even the smallest of the Small Vehicle and the stupidest of people could understand this Dharma.

The Avatamsaka is considered to belong to the Sudden Teaching although it is also a Gradual Teaching. The Agama Period is called the Storehouse Teaching.

3. The Vaipulya Period. Vaipulya, also Sanskrit, means "extensive," and during this period the Pervasive Teaching was expounded. The Vaipulya Teaching pervades the former Agama Teaching and the following Prajna Teaching. It is like curdled milk, good for children and adults. Both those of the Small Vehicle and those of the Great Vehicle can study the Sutras of this period. It is represented by the time between nine and ten in the morning when the sun shines on the high peaks and on the level ground.

4. The Prajna Period. Prajna is the Separate Teaching and it is a means of entry into the Great Vehicle. Prajna is called the Separate Teaching because it is separate from the Pervasive Teaching of the Vaipulya Period which precedes it and also separate from the Perfect Teaching of the Lotus-Nirvana Period which follows it. The Separate Teaching can be compared to butter which is extracted from curdled milk and suitable for adults. It is also like the period from ten until eleven in the morning when the sun shines upon the entire earth and is approaching, but has not yet reached, the noon position.

Prajna is a Sanskrit word. Because it has three meanings it is considered a term with "many meanings." Prajna is therefore not translated but kept in the original language. There are three kinds of Prajna, literary, contemplative, and real mark.

A. Literary Prajna. Literary Prajna refers to Sutras, Shastras, and the Vinaya. It is transcendental literature; it is most certainly not the literature of the world. Knowledge gained through mundane writings is not Prajna, but only worldly intelligence and cleverness.

B. Contemplative Prajna. Contemplative Prajna means that through the use of wisdom one regards and illuminates all dharmas. As it says in the *Heart Sutra*, "When the Bodhisattva Avalokiteshvara was practicing the deep Prajna-paramita, he illumined and viewed the five heaps all as empty..."

C. Real Mark Prajna. The Real Mark is unmarked and yet it is complete with all marks; it includes all marks. All marks flow from the unmarked, and that is just the Real Mark Prajna.

By means of Literary Prajna, one gives rise to Contemplative Prajna. With Contemplative Prajna one in turn penetrates to the inherent Real Mark Prajna within one's own nature.

5. The Dharma Flower-Nirvana Period. This is the ultimate teaching of the Buddha, the teaching of the *Wonderful Dharma Lotus Flower Sutra*. Do not look lightly on the *Dharma Flower*. It is the Buddha's ultimate expression, the most final Dharma-door. The four preceding periods were all taught to pave the way for the *Dharma Flower Sutra*, and so it is said that the *Dharma Flower* opens the provisional and manifests the real. The teachings of the other four periods were "manifesting the provisional for the sake of the real. The dharmas contained within them were taught for the sake of the *Dharma Flower*. The *Dharma Flower* opens the provisional and manifests the real. It annuls the provisional and establishes the real, thus dispensing with all former expedient Dharma-doors.

The *Dharma Flower Sutra* is the Buddha's true mind. The *Dharma Flower Sutra* is the Buddha's true body. The *Dharma Flower Sutra* is the Buddha's Dharma-body. The *Dharma Flower Sutra* is the Buddha's Reward-body. The *Dharma Flower Sutra* is the Buddha's Response-body. Students of the Buddhadharma who have not thoroughly understood *The Dharma Flower Sutra* have not yet obtained the genuine taste of the Dharma. The genuine wonderful meaning of the Buddhadharma is contained within this Sutra and therefore it is said to be a "wonderful Dharma."

The Dharma of this Sutra is compared to the lotus, the king and most rare of flowers. The lotus grows from the mud but remains unsoiled. Although its roots are in the mud, it grows up through the water; while in the dirt, it transcends the dirt. The lotus flower is a wonderful lotus, a superb flower; this Sutra is the ultimate Sutra. It is said, "With the *Shurangama* one develops wisdom; with the *Dharma Flower* one becomes a Buddha." If you wish to realize Buddhahood, you must certainly study this Sutra.

In Buddhism, the *Dharma Flower* and the *Shurangama* occupy the most important positions, especially the *Dharma Flower*. All other Sutras were spoken for the sake of the *Dharma Flower* and so it is called "the king of Sutras." That we are now able to investigate this Sutra is an unspeakably wonderful opportunity.

The Dharma Flower Sutra may be compared to the sun at high noon which shines upon the entire earth--the high peaks, the deep valleys, and the level ground. This Sutra is the Dharma-door of "opening the provisional to manifest the real." For what one purpose did the Buddha come into the world? The Buddha manifested himself in the world expressly for the purpose of speaking *The Dharma Flower Sutra*. Now, we have a chance to listen to it and in the future we will come to thoroughly understand its wonderful principles. Thus, our very hearing of the Sutra indicates that we have planted good roots for limitless aeons which have now enabled us to meet this opportunity. This is an inconceivable Sutra and a most rare Dharma Assembly.

The Buddha lived for the purpose of speaking *The Dharma Flower Sutra* and we are now able to hear it. We should give rise to great joy! We should consider how rare it is. Think it over: In all the years since America became a nation, how many people have had a chance to properly and truly listen to *The Dharma Flower Sutra* or *The Shurangama Sutra*? No one. Some may have read translations, but that is like an ant nibbling at a watermelon. It runs around and around, nibbling here and there, but never tastes it. Reading Sutras on one's own is like the ant nibbling at the melon. The melon is sweet, but no matter how long the ant runs around on the outside, he has no way to get into it and taste its flavor. Now, we have opened the melon. We are people, not ants, and we can taste it.

According to the Five Flavor's Analogy, we have seen raw milk, coagulated milk, curdled milk, and butter used to represent the first four teaching periods, respectively. The fifth period, the Dharma-Flower Nirvana Period,

is likened to clarified butter, the finest and most subtle
of tastes. The teaching of *The Dharma Flower Sutra* is like
the wonderful taste of clarified butter, the world's most
delicious flavor--nothing tastes better.

Now, as we open *The Dharma Flower Sutra*, we can each
find out for ourselves just what that flavor is.

During the fifth period, both the *Dharma Flower* and
the *Nirvana* Sutras were spoken. The *Dharma Flower* took
eight years and the *Nirvana* took one day and one night.
The aim of the Buddha was to speak *The Dharma Flower Sutra*.
It is said to be "purely complete and solitarily wonderful." It is "purely complete" because it is the pure
Perfect Teaching and is not mixed with the Storehouse,
Pervasive, or Separate Teachings. It is only the Perfect Teaching. Thus, in Buddhism, *The Dharma Flower Sutra*
is the most important. Students of the Buddhadharma who
have not read, recited, or heard it certainly cannot be
said to understand the Buddhadharma. Why not? The
speaking of *The Dharma Flower Sutra* was the final goal of
the Buddha's life. If Buddhist disciples don't understand it, they don't understand Buddhism, for they have
not understood clearly the wonderful Dharma.

The Dharma Flower Sutra is like the blazing sun at
midday, shining on all the mountains, rivers, forests,
and plants. The hills and valleys all receive this
universal illumination. In the Dharma Flower Assembly
all are said to be destined for Buddhahood. In the
second chapter of the Sutra the Buddha says,

> "If people with scattered thoughts
> enter stupas or temples
> And say but once, 'Homage to the Buddha,'
> they will all realize the Buddha Way."

In this verse, Shakyamuni Buddha gives us all a
prediction of Buddhahood, saying, "He doesn't need to
be single-minded. If, with a scattered mind he goes
into a Buddhist pagoda or temple and says only once,
'Homage to the Buddha,' it is for certain that he will
become a Buddha."

Or perhaps a person merely raises his hand in
salute. Although this is a very disrespectful gesture,
if one waves his hand or merely nods his head, he will
accomplish Buddhahood. Those who bow to the Buddha and
recite the Buddha's name will certainly become Buddhas,
too.

You may think, "If one who merely raises his hand
or nods his head with a scattered mind is certain to
become a Buddha, then the merit and virtue accrued from
my sincere worship must indeed be great."

Do not hold such arrogant thoughts. Although it is

true that such people will become Buddhas, those who
understand the Buddhadharma must add sincerity to their
sincerity, and respect to their respect, and vigorously
pursue their study of the Dharma. Do not be self-satisfied and think, "If someone who merely nods his head
with a scattered mind will become a Buddha, well
then I don't need to cultivate in order to become a
Buddha." Don't have such self-satisfied thoughts.

Of the Four Teachings--Storehouse, Pervasive,
Separate, and Perfect--the Dharma Flower is the Perfect
Teaching. These four are called the Four Types of Teaching. There are also Four Methods of Teaching, the Sudden, Gradual, Secret, and Unfixed Teachings. Together,
there are Eight Teachings. The Four Types of Teaching
are like types of medicine and the Four Methods of
Teaching are like instructions on how the medicine is
to be administered. It is not enough merely to have
the medicine and know it will cure the illness. The
medicine must be used. After it has been administered,
the illness vanishes.

Now, I will discuss the Eight Teachings, starting
with the Four Methods of Teaching:

1. The Sudden Teaching. What is meant by "sudden?"
Sudden means "becoming a Buddha instantly." There is no
need to wait. One immediately becomes a Buddha. Living
beings who have roots in the Sudden Teaching instantane-
ously become enlightened. Sudden means "very fast." The
Sixth Patriarch taught the Sudden Teaching and the
Gradual Teaching was taught by the Great Master Shen
Hsiu.

2. The Gradual Teaching. Gradual refers to cultivation by degrees. Sudden means suddenly becoming enlightened and gradual means to become enlightened slowly
and gradually.

3. The Secret Teaching. The Secret Teaching taught
by the Buddha refers to mantras. Secret means "taught
to one person and the other doesn't know; taught to the
other person and that person doesn't know; each is un-
aware of the teaching the other has received." Thus, it
is secret.

4. The Unfixed Teaching. The Dharma is taught in
an unfixed manner. *The Vajra Sutra* says, "Dharmas must
be relinquished, how much the more so that which is
not Dharma?" There are no fixed, static dharmas. Because it is not fixed, the Dharma is alive. Dharma
which is alive is separate from all attachments. So it
is said, "One bestows the teaching for the sake of the
individual and prescribes the medicine according to the
illness." According to the person's needs, one pre-

scribes a certain drug. In the same way, the Dharma is
spoken to counteract an individual's specific problems.

Thus together there are Eight Teachings which were
taught in the Five Periods. The Five Periods are also
known as 1) the sunrise period, 2) the period of bright
illumination, 3) the period of reflective illumination,
4) the period of level illumination, and 5) the period
of high noon. The final period is the Lotus-Nirvana
period and during this time there were not even any
shadows.

The Five Periods and the Eight Teachings encompass
all of the Dharma the Buddha spoke. After realizing
Buddhahood, the Buddha taught the Dharma for forty-nine
years in over three hundred Dharma assemblies, and it
was all for the sake of *The Dharma Flower Sutra*. When he
spoke the *Avatamsaka*, those with the dispositions of the
Small Vehicle were unable to accept it. Later, he "hid
the great and manifested the small." No longer did he
expound the lofty, profound theories, but instead he
spoke the superficial Agama doctrines, to lead those of
the Two Vehicles towards the Great Vehicle. After he
spoke the Agamas, the Buddha spoke the Vaipulya Teaching.
Progressing step by step, he next taught the Prajna
Teachings so that his listeners might gain wisdom. With
wisdom, they would be able to graduate to the wonderful
Dharma of *The Dharma Flower Sutra*.

However, *The Dharma Flower Sutra* is extremely difficult
to encounter, extremely difficult to hear. When the
Buddha spoke this Sutra, five thousand of his disciples
stood up and walked out. As soon as they heard the
Buddha speak it they thought, "This Dharma is utterly
unbelievable; we cannot believe it." Think of it: When
Shakyamuni Buddha spoke the *Dharma Flower*, five thousand
of his own disciples ran off. From this we can see that
it is very difficult to believe.

For this reason, when the Buddha spoke this Sutra
he said, "Stop! Stop! I will not speak. I won't speak
The Dharma Flower Sutra. Why not? My Dharma is wonderful
and hard to understand. The Dharma of this Sutra is
extremely wonderful, hard to understand and these people
won't be able to believe it. It would be better if I
didn't speak it at all." However, Shariputra insisted
on asking Shakyamuni Buddha to speak the Sutra.

Shakyamuni Buddha labored for several decades, preparing to speak this Sutra. For the sake of the real
he first bestowed the provisional teachings, but those
provisional teachings were all given for the sake of the
wonderful doctrines of the Perfect Teaching, the Real
Mark, *The Dharma Flower Sutra*. The preceding Dharma

Assemblies--Agama, Vaipulya, and Prajna--were all spoken to pave the way for *The Dharma Flower Sutra.* This may be compared to building a road from San Francisco to New York. When the work begins, it is for the sake of eventually arriving in New York. After several years of hard work, the road is finished. But although it is completed, there will be those who will not want to go. "You wanted a road," they may say, "and now you've got it. But I'm not going." So it was with the five thousand who walked out.

Now, we are explaining *The Dharma Flower Sutra* and the entire universe will emit light; the Buddhas and Bodhisattvas of the ten directions are especially happy. We who investigate the Buddhadharma should take time from our busy schedules to come and hear the Buddhadharma. This is the most wonderful of all Sutras, and we should not pass up the chance to obtain "the wonderful." If you don't obtain the wonderful, it becomes "unwonderful." So, everyone should not remain "unwonderful," but should discover the wonderful. If you wish to obtain the wonderful, you must first put forth great effort and solidly persevere. Investigate the wonderful Dharma.

PART II.

The Five Profound Meanings

According to the *T'ien T'ai* School, before lecturing the Sutra proper, one first examines its principles by means of the Five Profound Meanings. The five are:
1. Explanation of the Title.
2. Discrimination of the Substance
3. Clarification of the Doctrine
4. Discussion of the Function, and
5. Determination of the Teaching-mark.

Explanation of the Title:

Sutra titles fall into seven classes according to their reference to person, dharma, and analogy as follows:
A. Three Single. Three of the seven classifications are established by reference to either a person, a dharma, or an analogy:
1. *The Buddha Speaks of Amitabha Sutra* is an example of a title established solely by reference to people: the Buddha and Amitabha. In this Sutra, Shakyamuni Buddha speaks of the Pure Western Land of Ultimate Bliss

of Amitabha Buddha. In the past, when Amitabha was cultivating on the causal ground, he was a Bhikshu named
Fa Tsang, "Dharma Treasury." At that time he made forty-
eight great vows, each one of which concerned taking living beings across the sea of suffering to rebirth in the
Land of Ultimate Bliss where they can cultivate and become Buddhas.
     This Sutra is extremely important, for in the Dharma-
ending age it will be the last to disappear. The first
Sutra to become extinct will be *The Shurangama Sutra*. *The
Shurangama Sutra* explains all the affairs of the world in
great detail and exposes the secrets of heaven and earth.
After it becomes extinct, all the other Sutras will pass
out of existence one by one until only *The Amitabha Sutra*
remains. When *The Amitabha Sutra* has become extinct, only
the phrase, "Namo Amitabha Buddha" will remain in the
world one hundred years more. Then only the words
"Amitabha Buddha" will remain yet another one hundred
years to save living beings. After that, the Buddhadharma will disappear from the human realm. There won't
be many people left in the world then, either. The three
disasters--flood, fire, and wind--and the eight diffi-
culties, and all manner of calamities will arise and
completely destroy the world.
     We should pay attention to *The Amitabha Sutra* because,
in the Dharma-ending age, the Pure Land Dharma-door will
be the most suitable for saving people.
     The Orthodox Dharma age, however, may be found right
within the Dharma-ending age. For example, the Dharma is
just now being transmitted to American and people are
hearing it for the first time; you could say it is the
Orthodox Dharma age. In America many people like to sit
in meditation and investigate the Dharma and the customs
of Buddhism are gradually being introduced.
     2. *The Mahaparinirvana Sutra* is a title established
solely by reference to a dharma; Nirvana is the dharma
of neither production nor extinction.
     3. *The Brahma Net Sutra* is a title established
solely by reference to an analogy. The Brahma net is
a great circular net curtain which hangs in the heaven
of the Great Brahma King, who is fond of such adornments.
Within each hole in the net there is a gem which emits
light by day and by night. The light of every gem is
reflected in every other gem and the spaces in the net
interpenetrate. In that Sutra the Buddha explains the
Bodhisattva precepts. If you keep the precepts, you will
emit light, like the gems in the Brahma King's net.
     B. Three Paired.
     4. *The Sutra of the Questions of Manjushri* is a title

established by reference to a person, Manjushri, and the Dharma he requested, Prajna. Because Manjushri was the Bodhisattva of great wisdom, he could ask about Prajna, the dharma of wisdom.

5. *The Sutra of the Lion's Roar of the Thus Come One* is a Sutra established by reference to a person and an analogy. The Lion's Roar is an analogy for his speaking of Dharma. When the lion roars, all the wild beasts are terrified. Wolves, bears, and panthers are so frightened that they don't know what to do.

6. *The Wonderful Dharma Lotus Flower Sutra* is a title established with reference to a dharma and an analogy; the Wonderful Dharma is like the Lotus Flower.

C. Three-in-One. The seventh classification contains references to person, dharma, and analogy.

7. *The Great Universal Buddha Flower Adornment Sutra* refers to the Buddha as a person, Great and Universal as a dharma, and Flower Adornment as an analogy.

Those who study the Dharma must be able to explain these seven classifications from memory. The Buddhist scriptures number in the thousands, but there is not one of them that cannot be classified by its title into one of the seven above. When you study a Sutra, you should know how its title is classified. You may then deeply enter the Sutra storehouse. Having deeply entered the Sutra storehouse, you may have wisdom like the sea. If you don't even recognize the title, what use is it to study the Sutra? It's like saying, "I have a very good friend. We get along quite well."

"Really?" someone asks. "What is his name?"

"I don't know!" you say. What kind of good friend is he if you don't even know his name? And if you don't know his name, how could you know where he lives or what he does? The same is true of the principles in the Sutras. If you don't understand the title, you won't be able to enter deeply the Sutra storehouse and have wisdom like the sea. If you don't have wisdom like the sea, you may study the Dharma all your life, and you'll still be just as confused. So, the Seven Sutra Title Classifications are very important and everyone should know them. Then they may really investigate the Dharma.

Getting to know a Sutra is like getting to know a person. First, you learn his name; this corresponds to the Explanation of the Title. Then you learn to recognize him on sight. Is he tall or short? What does he look like? Is he healthy? This corresponds to the Discrimination of the Substance. Then, you discover his basic principles. Is he a businessman? Is he a student?

In general, what are his interests? This is the Clarification of the Doctrine.

Suppose he is a student. What function does he serve? Does he simply study and then go to sleep? No doubt he will develop his talents and become a useful member of society, as scientist or perhaps a philosopher. This is the Discussion of the Function.

Finally, knowing the above, you will be able to identify him as a professor, an engineer, or an educator, and you will be able to determine just what his accomplishments in life will be. This corresponds to the Determination of the Teaching Mark.

According to the Seven Title Classifications explained above, this Sutra is established by reference to a dharma and an analogy. The Wonderful Dharma is a dharma and the Lotus Flower is an analogy. Because the Wonderful Dharma is difficult to understand, the Lotus is used as an analogy.

The Wonderful Dharma

Ultimately, how wonderful is the wonderful dharma? It cannot be thought of and it cannot be expressed in words. You may try to comprehend it, but no matter how much you think, you won't understand it, for once you understand it, it's no longer wonderful. It is inconceivable and unthinkable, how much the less can it be spoken of? But you can't just say, "It's ineffable," and leave it at that; you still must speak of it. The speaking itself is not wonderful, but merely describes the wonderful. Ultimately, the genuine wonder is something known only to the Buddhas. Only the Buddhas can clearly understand this state.

Common people may claim, "I understand *The Wonderful Dharma Lotus Flower Sutra!*" but what do they mean by that? The wonderful dharma is just that which cannot be understood.

"If it cannot be understood," you may ask, "then what's the use of lecturing on it?" We will explain a small part of its meaning, not its entire meaning. It would simply be impossible to explain the entire scope of the meaning of the word "wonderful." I couldn't do it. I'm being quite frank and open on this point. I don't go around saying, "I understand," and explaining things I know nothing about. Such behavior is just cheating others and cheating oneself as well. So now I will explain only a little bit of *The Wonderful Dharma Lotus Flower Sutra*. However, I don't know how long it will take me to explain even this little bit. It took the Great

Master *Chih-che* of the *T'ien T'ai* School ninety days to
lecture on the one word "wonderful." During the past
Summer (1968) I took ninety-six days to explain *The
Shurangama Sutra* and that is really rocket-speed. In
Hong Kong, it took me fourteen months to explain *The
Shurangama Sutra*. In ninety days, Great Master *Chih-che*
did not finish explaining the word "wonderful." He only
explained a small part of it.

Now, let's talk about he word "wonderful." How
many days will it take to explain it? I haven't figured
it out in advance. It will take however long it takes.

What is "wonderful?" The wonderful dharma is wonderful. Living beings are wonderful. What is wonderful?
The Buddha is wonderful. There is nothing within heaven
and earth that is not wonderful. Tell me, what is not
wonderful? Everything is the wonderful dharma, and the
possibilities for explaining the word "wonderful" are
unlimited.

You may say, "This is wonderful and that is wonderful, but where does the wonderful come from?"

I will tell you: The wonderful comes from the heart.
How is it that you know it is a wonderful dharma? It is
because you have a heart. Because the dharma of the
heart is wonderful, the dharma of living beings is also
wonderful. The Buddhadharma is wonderful, too.

How is the dharma of the heart wonderful? All of
the mountains and rivers and the earth with its vege-
tation and dwellings--where does it come from? It all
comes from the present thought manifest in the hearts
of every one of us. How do the thoughts arise from the
heart?

"I don't know," you say.

Your "not knowing" is wonderful!

"I do know," you say.

Then, your "knowing" is also wonderful. Both
knowing and not knowing are wonderful. Why? Could
your not knowing be anything but wonderful? Could your
knowing be anything but wonderful?

You ask, "How can the heart be wonderful?"

Most people think of their heart as being a lump
of flesh inside their chest, but that is to mistake a
thief for your son, like Ananda who, in *The Shurangama
Sutra*, held that his mind was inside his body. That
heart is nothing but a lump of flesh and it is useless.
It is called the "heart which arises because of accumu-
lation," for it comes into being from the massing of
afflictions. It is also called the "conditioned and
considering heart" because it is able to work conditions to its own advantage and to consider matters.

This heart is the sixth (mind) consciousness. It is responsible for our false-thinking and scattered thoughts. Such is the fleshy heart; it goes by many names. Do not think that the heart-Dharma which I am explaining refers to this false-thinking heart.

"Do you mean to say that I have another heart?" you ask.

You mean you didn't know? Isn't that wonderful? You don't even know about your own heart! That really is wonderful. If you don't even know about your heart, how could you understand your own life? You come into the world in a confused daze--that confused daze is also wonderful. You leave the world in a stupor and understand nothing. You don't understand how you got here and, when it comes time to die, you leave all muddled, with no idea of where you are going. This, too, is wonderful. But coming and going, you don't understand.

You reply, "Dharma Master, you have said that birth and death are wonderful and I grant that they are. However, the duration of my life itself is not very wonderful."

Your life is even more wonderful. Why? Without being aware of it, a child grows into young adulthood; the young adult then becomes a grown-up. Without being aware of what is happening, the grown-up grows into an old man. Is this not wonderful? Not only does he become and adult, but he gives birth to many sons and daughters. If it is not wonderful, how, without one's even being aware of them, could so many changes take place?

Perhaps you find my explanation of the wonderful dharma to be meaningful and admit, "The Dharma Master says this is wonderful dharma, and it certainly must be so." But before I explained the wonderful dharma, you didn't know it was wonderful. The wonderful dharma refers to, right within one's not knowing, within that unawareness, nonetheless acting according to the wonderful dharma. *That's* wonderful. There's no end to speaking about the wonderful dharma.

What is right in front of you is wonderful. Your ability to see it is also wonderful. If it were not wonderful, you couldn't see.

"Then," you ask, "is that which I cannot see *not* wonderful?"

What you cannot see is even more wonderful. Both what you see and do not see, hear and do not hear, is wonderful.

Not just the seeing itself, but the ability to see is also wonderful. The question of "seeing" is discussed

at length in *The Shurangama Sutra*. There it is asked, "Who
is it who is able to see? Who does the seeing?"

Why is it that you are able to see things nearby?

"Well, because they are nearby."

But isn't that wonderful? Why can't you see things
that are far away, but only things that are nearby?
Isn't that wonderful? When you see the color yellow, an
impression of the color yellow is created in the field
of your eighth consciousness. The same applies to seeing other colors--green, red, white, or black. How is
the impression created? On whose instructions is the
impression created? No one's, and *that* is wonderful.
There's no one standing next to you saying, "Now, you
are seeing yellow; the yellow impression should arise
within your mind." You do it yourself. Isn't this
wonderful?

Your ability to create these impressions is wonderful, isn't it? Hearing works in the same way. Why do
some sounds please us and others annoy us? Who instructs you to like or dislike them? No one. Then why
do some sights delight you and others repulse you? Why
do you give rise to liking and disliking? Some forms we
find beautiful and give rise to craving for; others we
find ugly and are repulsed by. Who instructs us to do
this?

"I don't know who tells me to do it. I just think
that way," you say.

You just think that way, and that is wonderful.
So everything, everything is wonderful dharma. The
heart-dharma is wonderful and, from within the heart, a
thousand changes and myriad transformations arise. Could
this happen if it were not wonderful?

Actually, I could talk about the wonderful for several hundred years and never finish. If I finished, it
would not be wonderful. It's just because there's no end
to speaking of it that it is wonderful. Shakyamuni
Buddha taught the Dharma for forty-nine years in over
three hundred Dharma Assemblies and never went beyond the
wonderful. The word wonderful, then, includes the entire Tripitaka with its Twelve Types of Sutra Text. The
word wonderful includes all of the Buddhadharmas; not
one of them goes beyond it. Isn't this wonderful?

Great Master *Chih-che* took ninety days to speak about
the word wonderful, but really, one couldn't finish in
ninety years.

"Wow," you say, "in that case there's certainly not
enough time in one life to hear the entire Sutra explained. Better not listen."

Don't worry. In the atomic age everything happens

fast. Lecturing on the Sutra fast is also wonderful.
Faster or slower, it's still wonderful. If Shakyamuni
Buddha did not lecture beyond the wonderful, how could I
now stray from the wonderful?

Although the Dharma is wonderful, if we wish to
understand it, we must put down our attachments. If you
don't put them down, it's still wonderful, but if you do
put them down, it's even more wonderful. If you don't
believe me, try it out. Put down both your body and
your mind so that,

Inwardly, there is no body and mind;
Outwardly, there is no world.

When people and dharmas are empty--when all is completely empty--could this be anything but wonderful? To obtain the genuine wonder which is inherent within the
self-nature of us all, everything must be put down. Inwardly, you have no body and mind, and, outwardly, there
is no world, and yet you still have not separated from
the body and mind and the world. It is not the case
that, in order to be without body, mind, or world, you
must separate from the body, mind or world. It is
right within the body and mind, right within the world,
that they do not exist. I often say,

The eyes view external forms
but inside there is nothing.
The ears hear mundane sounds,
but the mind does not know.

Such an accomplishment is not easy. It is, in fact, extremely difficult, and so it is wonderful. What is easy
is also wonderful. It is *all* wonderful. Everything is
wonderful; nothing goes beyond the wonderful dharma. No
wonder   Great Master *Chih-che* took ninety days to explain it. There's no way one could ever finish explaining it. No way.

The wonderful dharma is difficult to speak of. Because it is difficult to speak of, it is wonderful. As
difficult as it is, still, we shall speak of it, and
that, in itself, is wonderful. No matter how you explain the wonderful, it's wonderful. In general then:
wonder, wonder, wonder, wonder--everything is wondrous,
filled with wonder, and wonderful.

You ask, "As wondrous, filled with wonder, and wonderful as it is, ultimately what is the function of this
wonder?"

And your asking that question is also truly wonderful! One cultivates and practices Dhyana meditation in
order to find this wonder. Seeking the wonderful,
Shakyamuni Buddha practiced ascetic practices in the
Himalayas for six years. Seeking the wonderful, the

Bodhisattvas cultivate the Bodhisattva Way. The Arhats put everything else aside to seek the wonderful. The common people cultivate the Way seeking the wonderful. Sages also cultivate seeking the wonderful. The position of Buddhahood is called "wonderful enlightenment." The highest level of Bodhisattva attainment is called "equal enlightenment," and it is not as high as "wonderful enlightenment." Only the Buddhas have attained wonderful enlightenment.

So we must understand the wonderful. What function does it have? It has no function at all. It is entirely useless and yet everything depends upon it. Speaking of the great function, the great creative power, of the wonderful, you might say,

Let it go,
and it fills the universe.

Born from the wonderful are heaven, earth, and all creation. Do not hold the mistaken notion that god, or people, created the universe. It was created from the wonderful. Only the Buddhas can truly understand the wonderful. The inherent Buddha nature is called the Buddha nature of wonderful enlightenment.

Perhaps you think, "I can't expect it to be easy to understand the wonderful; if it were easily understood, it wouldn't be called "wonderful."

But, again, you are wrong. If you could easily and effortlessly understand the wonderful that would be even more wonderful. To exert great effort to understand is also wonderful; however, no matter what you say about it, it is wonderful:

In all directions, it's the Way;
To the left and right, one meets the source.

What do you see that is not wonderful? The lamps, chairs, tables--everything, absolutely everything--is a manifestation of the wonderful dharma. If you understand the wonderful dharma, then everything is wonderful. If you don't understand the wonderful dharma, then all dharmas are "unwonderful," and, although you may think that you understand them clearly, actually you don't understand them at all. If you look deeply into their basic substance, you will find that they all arise from the wonderful.

Last Summer, I took ninety-six days to explain *The Shurangama Sutra*. In this Sutra there is a discussion of fifty kinds of demonic states associated with the five skandhas. All of these demonic states are higher than the states of present day "heavenly demons" and non-Buddhist religions. So, in giving a certain religion the title "ghostly and demonic," I am actually giving it

more credit than it is due. Members of this religion are
actually not as good as demons and ghosts. No doubt the
demons and ghosts wouldn't even take them for their
grandsons. But, because I am personally acquainted with
these people, I have given them the rather elevated
title of "demons and ghosts."

The wonderful functioning of the spiritual powers of
the fifty skandha demons is extremely powerful. Some of
them can emit light from the top of their heads and then
transfer it to your head so that your head also emits
light. In Buddhism, however, such spiritual powers are
considered demonic. So people who cannot even emit
light cannot rightly be called demons. They are more
like houseflies. They buzz north, east, south, and
west, back and forth, but they can't find their way out.
The blind followers are just like that. "Blind followers" are those who cultivate the Way under the guidance
of a blindman. If you don't understand, you should
study a religion that will teach you how to understand.
This particular religion's theories are riddled with
fallacies and its methods simply don't work and yet it
claims to incorporate all religions   In China we say,
"He slaps his face until it swells so that he can have
chubby cheeks." Ordinary people, without much understanding, are led astray by these blindmen. In the
world there are few people who possess understanding and
many who do not. Many are stupid, few have wisdom. Wise
people like to hear true principle; those without wisdom
listen to the teachings of those who confuse them and
lead them astray. I am not trying to insult anyone, but
those who follow this teaching do so because they do not
want to put an end to sexual desire. They want to do as
they please, and so they like this religion.   Buddhism
teaches the severing of sexual desire. As *The Shurangama
Sutra* states, cultivating the Way without cutting off
sexual desire is like cooking sand, hoping to get rice.
It's impossible. If you think you can enjoy both the
mundane pleasures of worldly desires and the ultimate
bliss of the transcendental as well, you are mistaken.
It cannot be done. You cannot have both.

There are some people who investigate the Buddhadharma, but they merely use their brains and mouths and
don't actually do the work. Because they do not rely
upon the methods taught by the Buddha in their practice,
they are like demons and cannot be called disciples of
the Buddha. Some people say that they believe in Buddhism
and yet they do not even bow to the Buddha. They are in
for some severe retribution. Whether they wind up as
animals, ghosts, or hell-beings cannot be known for sure.

Those who study the Buddhadharma must do so according to the methods taught by the Buddha. It's a serious mistake to see yourself as bigger than the Buddha. Students of the Dharma must revere not only the Budddha, but they should bow to the Bodhisattvas and Arhats as well, and to all those who have great goodness and cultivation. They must not be arrogant and proud and think of themselves as number one.

In the twentieth chapter of *The Dharma Flower Sutra*, the story of "Never-slighting Bodhisattva" is related. Who was "Never-slighting Bodhisattva?" He was a former incarnation of Shakyamuni Buddha. Cultivating the Bodhisattva Way, he exclusively practiced the Ten Great Kingly Vows of Samantabhadra Bodhisattva:

1. Worship and respect all Buddhas. One should respectfully bow to all the Buddhas of the past, present, and future, in the ten directions.

2. Praise the Thus Come Ones.

You ask, "Does the Buddha like people to praise him?"

That's a good question. Yes, he does. However, praising the Buddha is just praising yourself.

"But I don't want to praise myself," you say.

Then don't praise the Buddha, because the Buddha and living beings are one.

"Well, then, if I am a Buddha, I don't need to bow to the Buddha, do I?" you say.

Wrong again. Although your self-nature is the Buddha, you have not yet cultivated it, and so you are not yet identical with the Buddha and have not certified to the fruit. If everyone was a Buddha, then Shakyamuni Buddha would not have had to go to the Himalayas to meditate for six years and then sit beneath the Bodhi Tree for forty-nine days before becoming enlightened and realizing Buddhahood. He would not have had to toil so bitterly, would he? Shakyamuni Buddha cultivated all manner of bitter practices in former lives and all kinds of Dhyana samadhis. He practiced giving, morality, patience, vigor, and Prajna wisdom, too--all kinds of Dharma-doors. In his life as Shakyamuni Buddha, however, he still had to undertake ascetic practices in the Himalayas and sit beneath the Bodhi Tree where, finally one night, he saw a bright star and awoke to the Way. To say nothing of six years, you haven't even sat in the Himalayas for six days or six hours. And you claim to be a Buddha? That's too much of a bargain. Your Buddha is really too inexpensive. So those who say that they are Buddhas are shameless, brazen, and outrageously impudent.

"Never-slighting Bodhisattva" never looked down on anyone. When he saw the Buddhas, he bowed.

When he saw Bodhisattvas, Arhats, Bhikshus, Bhikshunis, he also bowed, and he said, "I dare not slight you, for you will all become Buddhas. To slight you would be to slight the Buddha." His devotion was completely genuine, without the slightest trace of falsehood. As a result, he was reviled by Bhikshus of overwhelming arrogance. "You don't understand anything about the Buddhadharma," they said, "and yet you go about transmitting predictions at random." They screamed at him and they beat him. When he bowed, they kicked him. They even kicked his teeth out! Under these circumstances, most people would have certainly discontinued the practice of bowing, but instead of giving up, Never-slighting Bodhisattva began bowing at a distance. He bowed and, without waiting for the person to come near him, he quickly ran off. Such was the practice of Shakyamuni Buddha in a former incarnation as Never-slighting Bodhisattva.

Shakyamuni Buddha did not become a Buddha overnight. He practice the six perfections and the ten thousand conducts through many lifetimes. The sons and grandsons of demons now shamelessly say, "Everyone is a Buddha." Their speech is deviant and their practice is crooked. People who think they are the Buddha do not recognize the Buddha. This is like declaring yourself the Emperor or electing yourself President. Without an election or loyal supporters, no one will recognize you. Such people always end up in jail because they totally disregard the country's laws. In fact, they are not shown the least bit of courtesy and are somtimes even beheaded! In Buddhism, people like this are certain to fall into the hells, because they think that they are Buddhas, but instead of cultivating, they create offenses. They use the Buddha's name to cheat and swindle people. "I am Buddha, and so are you," they say, "and we should do this and that." They devise schemes to cheat the world. Don't take it lightly; it's no game. It's more dangerous than sleeping every night with an atom bomb in your embrace. People who act this way are destined for no place but the hells. It is said,

> There are roads to the heavens,
> > but you don't walk them;
> Hell has no gate,
> > but you barge right in.

Another verse goes:

> One confused transmits that confusion;
> In one transmission, two misunderstand.
> The teacher plummets into the hells;
> His disciples follow, with their
> > hats in their hands.

When the disciples arrive, the teacher says, "What are you doing here?"

"We're your students," they say, "and of course we want to follow you."

"But you've made a terrible mistake. This is hell!"

"Oh no!" the students cry. "Why have you led us here?"

"I don't even know how *I* got here!" he cries. "But it's too late now. I can't get out."

Pathetic, isn't it? Not only the teacher, but all of his disciples are like fish trapped in a net. When will they get out? No one knows. No one has a solution for their problem. This is what happens when you claim to be a Buddha without recognizing the Buddha or understanding the Dharma. Such is the retribution incurred.

We were discussing the Ten Great Kingly Vows...

3. To cultivate extensively the giving of offerings. This is not to make offerings today and not make them tomorrow, to give to one Buddha and not another.

4. To repent and reform of karmic obstacles.

5. To follow along and rejoice in acts of merit and virtue. When you see a chance to do something good, you should do it. If you can do a penny's worth, do a penny's worth. If you can do a dollar's worth, do a dollar's worth. If you can do a hundred dollar's worth, do a hundred dollar's worth. Merit and virtue must be *done*, not just talked about. Practicing the Bodhisattva Way one must benefit others, not oneself. In general, those acts which help others and which are not done out of selfish, profit-seeking motives are all acts of "following along and rejoicing in merit and virtue."

6. To request the turning of the Dharma Wheel. This is to ask a Dharma Master to explain the Sutras. For example, a few days ago, some people requested me to lecture on *The Vajra Sutra*. Until now there has been no Buddhadharma in America and no one qualified to explain the Sutras. The Sutras are ineffably wonderful, and their wonderful doctrines cannot be understood without several decades of study and practice. In America a number of people say, "I am in Buddhist Studies, you know. I have a Doctorate in Buddhism." But if you haven't put your "self" down, you have not understood the Buddhadharma at all. If you understand the Buddhadharma, why do you still cling to your Ph.D.?

So the Ph.D.'s cheat little children. If you speak genuine principle, however, no one will listen. I explain genuine principle to you because you have reached a level where you can accept it. If I told everyone the truth right off, they would run in fright and never return. If you give a child a piece of candy, he will eat it and understand that it is sweet. If you try to reason with him, he simply won't understand, and if there is no candy to be had, he won't come back.

To request the turning of the Dharma Wheel is to ask those who truly understand the Buddhadharma to explain the Sutras, not just professors. If you want to be a carpenter, you should study with carpenters. If you want to be a metalworker, study with metalworkers. If you want to understand the Buddhadharma, then study with someone who really understands it;request the turning of the Dharma Wheel.

7. To request that the Buddhas dwell in the world. Now, the Buddha has entered Nirvana and no longer dwells in the world. Still, we can ask that the Buddhadharma remain in the world.

8. To follow the Buddha in study forever. When Shakyamuni Buddha practiced the Bodhisattva Way, he looked upon his own body as empty. We should follow his example.

9. To accord always with living beings. We should cooperate with living beings with the hope that they will gain understanding.

10. To dedicate all merit and virtue. All merit and virtue gained from one's own practices should be dedicated to the benefit of all living beings so that they may quickly realize the Buddha Way.

"Wonderful"

The first word of the Sutra's title is *Wonderful*, and this means its scope is extremely broad. Spoken horizontally, it is wonderful; spoken vertically, it is wonderful; spoken in great lands, it is wonderful; spoken in motes of dust, it is wonderful. All of the Dharma spoken by Shakyamuni Buddha is wonderful and the wonderful dharma includes the Three Divisions of the Tripitaka and the Twelve Types of Sutra Text.

The Three Divisions of the Tripitaka are:

1. The Sutra Division, which deals with the study of samadhi.

2. The Vinaya Division, which deals with the study of precepts, the moral code.

3. The Shastra Division, which deals with the study of wisdom.

These Three Divisions encompass limitless, boundless, unfathomable doctrines. The effective functioning gained through the practice of morality, samadhi, and

wisdom is also limitless and unbounded. For this
reason, the Sutras, Vinaya, and Shastras are wonderful
dharma and so are morality, samadhi, and wisdom.
    Although we hear a great deal about morality,
samadhi, and wisdom, we should ask ourselves just what
we are *doing* with respect to developing these   qualities.
Hearing the Dharma is not the same as understanding it.
To have any real attainment, one must at all times
renounce one's very body in order to cultivate. To
know and yet not cultivate is just the same as not
knowing. By way of example, you may know that something is delicious, but in order to really know, you
must go ahead and taste it. If you don't eat it, you
will never really know. The Buddhadharma works the
same way. If you know, but do not practice, you will
benefit neither yourself nor anyone else. To preach
without practicing is like being a person made of stone
whose body is so heavy he can only talk, he can't move
to actually do anything. True students of the Way
both talk and practice. The Dharma is to be taught and
the Way is to be practiced.

> You may speak of it wonderfully,
>   speak of it well,
> But unless you walk down it,
>   it's not the Way.

At all times, you must actually do the work.
    Within the Three Divisions of the Tripitaka, one
finds Twelve Types of Sutra Texts:

1. Prose.
2. Verse.
3. The transmitting of predictions.
4. Interjections.
5. Dharma spoken without request.
6. Causes and conditions.
7. Analogies.
8. Expanded (Vaipulya) writings.
9. Stories of the past lives of the Buddha.
10. Stories of the past lives of the Disciples.
11. Previously inexistent teachings.
12. Commentarial literature.

    Although it is important to remember points of
Buddhist doctrine and to know how to explian the lists
and terms, Buddhism isn't just concerned with scholarly
erudition. In Buddhism, the emphasis is placed upon
actual practice, the application of the principles and
attainment of true skill. For example, the Sixth Patriarch in China, the Great Master Hui Neng, never went
to school and couldn't even write his own name, and yet
he was able to lecture on the Sutras and teach the Dharma.

Other people would read the text aloud and he would explain it, sentence by sentence. He perfectly accorded with the principles of the Buddhas and never strayed from the Buddhadharma's meaning. Why was he able, as an illiterate, to explain the Sutras? It was because he had obtained the wonderful dharma of the Mind Seal of the Buddhas and Patriarchs and so the Dharma he spoke was wonderful dharma. After the Sixth Patriarch obtained the Mind Dharma from the Fifth Patriarch, and the robe and bowl, he dwelt with hunters for sixteen years. During that time he worked hard at his cultivation and developed great wisdom. However, this involves bitter toil. You can be nervous and try to rush. If you try to go too fast, you won't attain your goal. Cultivation is like shooting an arrow. If you pull the bowstring too tight, it will snap, but if it is too slack, the arrow won't fly. It is said,

> Go too fast and you'll trip;
> Dally and you'll fall behind.
> Never rush and never dally,
> And you'll get there right on time.

It is also said,

> A mad rush forward means a hasty retreat.

If you hurry in, you'll hurry out as well. Hasty progress means hasty regress. Don't be like the mayfly, born in the morning and dead by dusk--born fast and dying fast. Cultivate with honest and steady effort. Go down the main road and don't take short cuts. The main road is the six perfections and the ten thousand conducts. The short cuts are the non-Buddhist religions that promise quick progress when in reality they take you nowhere. Insist on cultivating the Way in accord with orthodox methods. That is the wonderful dharma. The Middle Way is the wonderful dharma.

One Thought of Arrogance

In China, during the Han Dynasty, there was an official named Yüan-nang who, out of jealousy, murdered another official named Ch'ao-ts'o. Later, day and night, he saw the ghost of Ch'ao-ts'o coming to kill him and he realized his mistake and left the home-life to become a Bhikshu. After he left home, the ghost quit bothering him.

He then resolutely cultivated Dhyana meditation and practiced the Way. Because he never met the ghost again during his life he made a vow: "I murdered a person," he said. "I vow that in my future life I will again be a monk and not an official." Accordingly, in his next

life, he was a monk. Not only was he a monk, he was a
great Dharma Master who went everywhere to lecture on
the Sutras. He did not seek fame or profit, either, but
cultivated intensely and coveted nothing. During all
this time he met no more ghosts. In this way he passed
through ten lifetimes and accumulated a bit of virtue.
In every life he rose higher and higher until, in his
tenth life as a Bhikshu, he became a National Master,
the Emperor's teacher.

One day, the Emperor presented him with a seat of
carved aloeswood. It was a priceless gift, for ordin-
arily only the Emperor could sit in such a seat. No one
else had the status, not even the highest ranking
officials. When the National Master sat in his beautiful
carved chair, he got a bit carried away. He thought,
"How many Dharma Masters are there like me? Are there
any as high? The Emperor sent me this chair, this wonderful chair..." Arrogantly, he figured, "In the heavens
and on the Earth, I alone am honored." Although this is
what the Buddha said when he was born, the National Master was *not* a Buddha. That single thought of arrogance
laid him open for an attack by the ghost of Ch'ao-ts'o
which had been following him around for the past ten
lifetimes. What do you think happened? His leg immediately broke out with a sore, and no ordinary sore it
was. It looked like a human face! It had eyes, ears,
a nose, and a mouth and could even talk. It demanded
to be fed and would only eat meat. Unless a piece of
meat was placed on it, it would be unbearably painful.
It would talk to the National Master, too, saying, "You
want to get away from me, but you can't. You'll never
get away because I am determined to take your life."
The National Master, whose name was Wu-ta, was helpless.
He recited the Shurangama Mantra and the Great Compassion
Mantra, but because his karmic obstacles were so heavy,
he got no response. His arrogant thought had caused the
Dharma Protectors to refuse to guard him and allowed the
vengeful ghost to gain hold. So his mantras didn't work.
It wasn't that the mantras didn't work, exactly, but
his karmic obstacles were just too overpowering.

Luckily, before he got the sore, National Master
Wu-ta had taken care of the Venerable Kanaka when his
entire body had broken out in filthy sores which stank,
ran with pus, and were crawling with worms. National
Master Wu-ta nursed the Venerable Kanaka back to health,
feeding him and preparing medicinal broths for him. But
was the Venerable Kanaka really ill? No. He deliberately
appeared to be sick in order to set up conditions to
save National Master Wu-ta. When he was well, the Ven-

erable Kanaka said to Wu-ta, "In the future, no matter
what great difficulty you run into, no matter what in-
solvable problem, you may come to see me in Szechwan,
to such and such a place, and I will think of a way to
help you." So when he realized he had no way to cure
his sore, National Master Wu-ta went to Szechwan to see
the Venerable Kanaka.

When Wu-ta arrived, the sore spoke to the Venerable
Kanaka, "You are a sage who has transcended the world
and you cannot act unreasonably. In a former life,
this man killed me and I have come to take revenge. If
you use your Dharma power to get rid of me, you're
being unfair."

The Venerable Kanaka said, "It's not a matter of
justice. I am going to liberate you as well and you
will also obtain advantage." Then the Venerable
Kanaka washed the sore with samadhi water and the sick-
ness was immediately cured.

We who cultivate the Way, no matter what, must
never be arrogant.

Living Beings Dharma/ Buddhadharma/ Heart Dharma

The dharma of living beings is wonderful; the
Buddhadharma is wonderful, and the heart-dharma is
wonderful. The heart-dharma is just the living beings-
dharma; the living beings-dharma is just the Buddhadharma; the Buddhadharma is just the heart-dharma.
These three dharmas are one dharma; the one dharma is
three dharmas. Why do I say this? Because it is wonderful.

What are living beings? They are the collective
body of all creatures who have a lifespan. There are
twelve groups of living beings: 1) egg-born, 2) womb-
born, 3) moisture-born, 4) transformationally-born,
5) those with form, 6) those without form, 7) those with
thought, 8) those without thought, 9) those formless
yet having form, 10) those having form and yet formless,
11) those having thought, yet thoughtless, 12) those
thoughtless, yet having thought.

Each of these twelve groups also has many subdiv-
isions. For example there are many different kinds of
beings born from eggs. Some beings born from eggs can
fly and some cannot, and of the egg-born beings who can
fly, there are thousands of different species. No one
could ever determine exactly how many different species
there are. Isn't this wonderful? Of course, if you
could determine the number, that would also be wonderful. The same applies to the eleven remaining groups.

Take, for example, beings born from wombs. Human beings are born from wombs and so are animals. *The Shurangama Sutra* discusses the twelve groups in detail. It says, "Beings born from eggs are born because of thought; beings born from wombs are born because of emotion." Everyone assumes that the emotion of love is extremely blissful. In reality, within this extreme bliss, the most painful of events takes place. In America, a lot of people have awakened to the fact that the emotion of love involves a lack of freedom. However, they misunderstand the underlying principle and go to the opposite extreme. In their quest for freedom, they become promiscuous. Their new-found "freedom" is just a mistake on top of a mistake. Although marriage limits one's freedom, it still fulfills the most primary relationship among human beings. To refuse to take on the responsibility of marriage and indulge in casual sexual relationships will ruin one's body and hasten one's death. If this situation is not quickly remedied, it will cause great harm to society.

Animals are also born because of emotions. Emotions come from habits deeply ingrained throughout limitless aeons. If, as a person, one's emotion and desire is weighty, one will fall into the realm of animals where, heavily burdened with emotion and desire, one will still not wake up. Moisture-born beings and transformationally-born beings are also born because of desire. In fact, in some sense, all beings are born because of emotion. It is said,

The true Buddha has ended karma
and emptied all emotions.
The living being has heavy karma
and confusing emotions.

Common people are deluded by their emotions. If you can see emotions as empty, that is sagehood. There are thousands of different kinds of beings, and yet, of all the twelve groups, not a single one is excluded from the wonderful dharma. All are included within the living beings-dharma. Therefore, the living beings-dharma is also wonderful.

Once you look into it, you will realize that each class of creature has its own reason for being. Why are people people? Why are dogs dogs? Why are pigs pigs? How does one become a horse or a cow? The wonderful dharma is behind it all.

You ask, "But why is there a wonderful dharma?" The reasons for all of these things are difficult to understand, and yet this difficulty is itself the wonderful dharma.

You say, "Well, I understand them."

Your understanding is also wonderful dharma. The wonderful dharma is an inconceivable state and this inconceivable state is just the way things are on the part of living beings.

Now, to discuss the wonder of the Buddhadharma. What is the Buddhadharma?

What is *not* the Buddhadharma?

All dharmas are the Buddhadharma. There is not a single dharma which is not the Buddhadharma.

How many Buddhadharmas are there?

In general, there are eighty-four thousand Dharma-doors.

Which of the eighty-four thousand Dharma-doors is the most wonderful?

All of them are the most wonderful.

Once, I answered this question by saying, "Whichever Dharma-door is of no use to you is the least important. Whichever Dharma-door suits you best is the most important." It depends on your disposition. The eighty-four thousand Dharma-doors were taught as antidotes for the eighty-four thousand afflictions and problems of living beings. If you have no problems, then none of the Dharma-doors are useful for you. If you still have troubles, however, if you are beset with affliction and ignorance, then whichever door cures your disease is the foremost Dharma-door. Therefore, there are eighty-four thousand Dharma-doors and eighty-four thousand of them are number one; eighty-four thousand are the highest and the most supreme.

Now, speaking in terms of the wonder of the Buddhadharma, I will tell you that, of the eighty-four thousand Dharma-doors, eighty-four thousand of them are the most wonderful. Why do I say this? *The Vajra Sutra* says, "The Dharma is level and equal, with nothing above or below it." All the Dharmas are like prescriptions written to cure specific illnesses. A good prescription will cure you; a wrong prescription may injure you. When used incorrectly, good medicine turns into deadly poison.

(A note on eating meat...)

Today, a guest asked, "Can you eat meat and still become enlightened?"

I told him, "If you can eat a whole cow, pig, or sheep in a single gulp, it might be possible to become enlightened as a meat-eater. If you have to eat them bite by bite, no one will guarantee an enlightenment. If you manage to swallow the animal whole, I will personally guarantee that you can become enlightened.

The Great Master the Sixth Patriarch lived with hunters for sixteen years and the hunters, of course, ate meat. The Sixth Patriarch ate "vegetables cooked alongside the meat." He grew vegetables on the mountain and cooked them right in the pot with the hunters' meat. When the stew was cooked, his vegetables were also ready. The Sixth Patriarch had already become enlightened. He was a Patriarch and so he could have eaten meat; he could have eaten anything at all. Unless we have the wisdom of the Sixth Patriarch, unless we have become enlightened, we shouldn't be preoccupied with eating gourmet food. Besides, no matter how delicious the dish, once it gets in your stomach it starts to stink and loses its appeal entirely.

This has been a discussion of the wonder of the Buddhadharma.

The heart-dharma is also wonderful. The heart of human beings creates the Ten Dharma Realms and the Ten Dharma Realms do not go beyond the current thought in the hearts of human beings.

For example, an evil thought plants the cause for falling into hell. Another evil thought plants the cause for entering the realm of hungry ghosts. Yet another evil thought of hatred plants the cause for becoming an asura. A thought of stupidity plants the cause for turning into an animal. A good thought causes one to be born in the path of human beings. A thought to keep the five precepts and cultivate the ten good deeds creates the causes for being born in the heavens.

If you bring forth the resolve to cultivate the Dharma-door of the Four Holy Truths: suffering, origination, extinction, and the Way, you plant the cause for become a Sound Hearer Disciple. If you resolve to cultivate the Dharma-door of Twelve Conditioned Causes, you plant the cause for becoming a Condition-enlightened One. If you resolve to cultivate the six perfections and ten thousand conducts, you plant the cause for becoming a Bodhisattva. If you resolve to cultivate diligently all the Buddhadharmas and you aspire to Buddhahood, you plant the cause of realizing Buddhahood.

Within the Ten Dharma Realms, there are Four Sagely Realms:
1. The Buddhas.
2. The Bodhisattvas.
3. The Condition-enlightened Ones.
4. The Sound Hearers.
There are also Six Common Realms:

5. The gods.
6. The human beings.
7. The asuras.
8. The hell-dwellers.
9. The hungry ghosts.
10. The animals.
   The Four Sagely Dharma Realms plus the Six Common
Dharma Realms make up the Ten Dharma Realms. Where do
the Ten Dharma Realms come from? They come from the
thought manifest in the heart. Thus it is said that
the heart-dharma is wonderful. If the heart-dharma
wasn't wonderful, the living beings-dharma would not be
wonderful. If the living beings-dharma wasn't wonderful,
the Buddhadharma wouldn't be wonderful. But, because
the heart-dharma is wonderful, the living beings-
dharma is wonderful, and because the living beings-dharma
is wonderful, the Buddhadharma is wonderful.
   The Buddhas of the ten directions all do not go
beyond the thought presently manifested in our hearts.
The Bodhisattvas of the ten directions do not go beyond
the thought presently manifested in our hearts. The
same applies to the remaining eight Dharma Realms. None
go beyond that current thought.
   In China, the ancients had this to say about the
Chinese character for heart, which looks like this:

Three dots spread above,
   like stars;
Below, a hook, like the
   crescent moon.
Animals arise from it;
And Buddhahood comes
   from it, too.

   The Chinese character for "heart" also means
"mind," or "thought." The three dots on the top look
like stars in the sky. The hook underneath them looks
like the crescent moon. Animals, wearing fur coats and
capped with horns, arise from the heart. However,
although animals are created from a thought within the
heart, Buddhas are also made from the heart. It's not
a matter of trading one for the other. It's just a
matter of one single thought from the heart.
   The Avatamsaka Sutra says,
      If a person wants to understand
      The Buddhas of the three periods of time,
      He should contemplate the nature
         of the Dharma Realm:
      Everything is made only from the mind.

We shouldn't explain it too mysteriously. If it's too wonderful, no one will understand it. If it's not wonderful enough, everyone will ignore it. So, I will talk about something a bit less wonderful, that is, eating. When you're hungry, you think about eating. Your heart thinks, "It's time, it's definitely time for lunch! Let's see, what will I cook up today?" and you decide what to eat. Is this wonderful or not? Just how did you give rise to this thought? How did you come to think to eat lunch?

"I was hungry," you reply.

How did you get hungry? It was an inconceivable state. In general, if you don't discriminate, that is wonderful. When you have arrived at the state where you neither discriminate nor deliberate then:

> Inwardly, there's no body and mind;
> Outwardly, there's no world.
> One is then released
> From the senses and their objects.

The eye, ear, nose, tongue, body and mind no longer exist and forms, sounds, smells, tastes, and objects of touch and dharmas have perished. The attainment of this state is truly wonderful dharma. Not having attained this state does not exclude one from the wonderful dharma, however, because every movement, every action, and every word we say is all wonderful dharma. Explained profoundly, it is wonderful dharma; explained super- ficially, it is wonderful dharma. *Every single dharma* is wonderful dharma. It's all a matter of whether or not you understand it. If you understand, then all dharmas are wonderful dharma. If you don't understand, you could still call it wonderful dharma, but it's only the coarse aspect of it you are seeing.

This has been a discussion of the wonderful dharma, but there is really no way to finish explaining it. If you could explain it completely, it would no longer be wonderful dharma. If I wanted to continue, I could talk about the wonderful dharma for several years.

I will now relate a story to describe the wonderful dharma, so that you may gain some understanding of it:

The First Half

Long ago there was an official who believed in Buddhism and was able to recite from memory the first half of *The Dharma Flower Sutra*. He memorized and understood the first half on sight, but no matter what he did, he couldn't get the second half through his head. He couldn't understand it at all, to say nothing of being

able to memorize it. He was a lot like one of my disciples who recently said, "The Shurangama Mantra has
really got me beat. No matter how I study it, I can't
remember it." Don't look at the sea and heave a great
sigh. Don't think of the mantra like the great sea and
assume that you'll never be able to learn it. I will
teach you a method. Don't try to learn it by reading it
all at once. Do it sentence by sentence, line by line.
When you can remember the first line by heart, go on to
the next. Unless you remember that one line clearly,
don't go on to the next. For example, repeat, "Namo
sa dan two su chye dwo ye e la he di san myau san pu two
sye..." over and over until you can say it with your
eyes closed. Then go on to the next line. If you're
greedy to learn it all at once you won't be able to
swallow it in one gulp, just like the guest who wanted
to know if he could eat meat and become enlightened. I
told him that he could if he could eat a whole cow in a
single gulp. He didn't understand what I meant, however,
and just said, "I couldn't do it." If you can't, how do
you expect to get enlightened eating meat? Which Buddha
became enlightened eating meat? Which Patriarch became
enlightened eating meat? Which Bodhisattva became enlightened eating meat?

     "None of them," you say.

     Then why do you want to be so special and insist on
eating meat and getting enlightened? What kind of an
enlightenment is that? An enlightenment to carnivorism.
The retribution incurred by eating meat is fearsome.
If you like to eat the meat of other creatures, eventually they will take delight in eating your flesh. So
the guest didn't return tonight. Probably because
there's no meat here to eat and he figured he wouldn't
get enlightened. Besides, he reeked with wine...

     Back to learning the Shurangama Mantra. Don't try
to learn it all at once. That's like trying to eat a
whole cow at once. Learn the mantra bit by bit. Don't
be like the one who gazes at the sea and heaves a big
sigh, thinking, "So much water. How could I ever drink
it all?" Although the Shurangama Mantra is very long,
if you concentrate on it, you can learn it. So anyone
who wishes to leave home under me must be able to recite
it and the Great Compassion Mantra. Otherwise   I will
not accept them as left-home disciples.

     If you can memorize the Shurangama Mantra, I will
grant that you have somewhat of a sincere heart.   In
China, it normally takes six months to learn the mantra.
During the Summer Session one of my disciples went
without eating or sleeping in order to focus his atten-

tion on learning the mantra. This was an indication of
his sincerity. He made his stomach empty so that it
could hold the mantra. Really, though, I'm joking. You
don't have to quit eating to learn the mantra.

So, all dharmas are the wonderful dharma. I have
lectured for so many days on the wonderful dharma, and
yet my explanation is nowhere near as broad as that of
the Great Master *Chih-che*, who took ninety days to explain the single word "wonderful." The state of the
wonderful dharma is beyond deliberation and discrimination. In trying to memorize the Shurangama Mantra,
do not fall into deliberation and discrimination. The
more you discriminate, the harder it is to learn it.
The more you deliberate, the less you will understand it.
Don't think, "Why am I unable to learn the mantra?" Don't
think of anything at all! Just recite it. Recite it as
your duty and responsibility. Don't study it with
thoughts of discrimination and deliberation. Discrimination takes place in the sixth (mind) consciousness.
Deliberation is done exclusively by the seventh consciousness. In the *Shurangama Sutra* we read that Ananda
had this very problem. Why? Because he concentrated on
learning and neglected cultivation of samadhi. If you
want to memorize the Shurangama Mantra you must get rid
of deliberation and discrimination. Do not use your
conscious mind mind to study the Buddhadharma. Use
your true heart, which is just the wonderful dharma.

What is the wonderful dharma? What you know is
the wonderful dharma. What you do not know is also
wonderful dharma. The wonderful dharma is just "not
knowing."

"But if I don't know the wonderful dharma, how can
I study it?"

Just study that "not knowing." Not knowing what?
Not knowing false thinking; not knowing hatred; not
knowing stupidity or greed. Learn how "not to know."
Get rid of greed, hatred, and stupidity. *That* is wonderful. If you can't part with your greed, hatred, and
stupidity, that is the wonderful within the wonderful.
If you can renounce them, that is the wonderful within
the unwonderful.

We were talking about the official who could remember
the first half of *The Dharma Flower Sutra* after he had read
it only once, but although he read the second half liter-
ally thousands of times, he couldn't remember a word
of it. Thinking this rather wonderful, he finally went
to ask the Abbot of a nearby monastery, an enlightened
Master. As a high-ranking official, he received a
warm welcome and he asked the Abbot, "I sincerely believe

in the Buddhadharma. I am expecially interested in *The Dharma Flower Sutra*. However, although I could understand the first half, and memorized it after hearing it only once, the second half escapes me entirely. Why is this? Most Venerable Abbot, I beg for your instruction on this point."

The Abbot, who had use of the five eyes and the six spiritual penetrations, said, "I can tell you why, but you must promise not to get angry, because what I am about to tell you is the truth. I am not trying to insult you."

The official said, "Of course I won't get angry. If you explain the former causes and following effects behind my situation, how could I get angry?"

The Abbot continued, "In your past life you were an ox who plowed the fields in a monastery. Through your toil you established a great deal of merit for yourself. In that monastery, during the sixth month of every year the Sutras were set in the sun to air so that they would not be eaten by worms. You happened to lumber over and sniff one of the copies of *The Lotus Sutra*. But you only sniffed the first volume, and not the second. Because of the merit you established, you have now become an official. Don't think that officials are always human. Many of them have been horses and cows, sheep and pigs. Because you only sniffed the first volume, not the second, you are familiar with the first and not the second. Such is the cause and effect here."

Hearing this, the official redoubled his vigor in supporting the Buddhadharma and the Bodhimanda. Most likely he never became an ox again. That's a wonderful dharma, indeed. All he did was sniff the first volume of the Sutra and as a human was able to remember it. Why? I don't know. It's a wonderful dharma. If you insist on knowing why, you can't pin it down with scientific research. The only way to find out is to singlemindedly concentrate and apply effort to your cultivation. When you have obtained the five eyes and the six spiritual penetrations, you will understand the reasons, you will understand the wonderful dharma.

The Six Levels of Identity with the Buddha

We have been discussing the wonder of the heart-dharma, the wonderful of the living beings-dharma, and the wonder of the Buddhadharma. Now we shall discuss the wonderful dharma according to the *T'ien T'ai* doctrine of the Six Levels of Identity with the Buddha:

1. Identity with the Buddha in Principle.

2. Nominal Identity with the Buddha.
3. Identity with the Buddha in Contemplation and Practice.
4. Similar Identity with the Buddha.
5. Identity with the Buddha Through Partial Certification.
6. Absolute Identity with the Buddha.

1. Identity with the Buddha in Principle.
What is the wonderful dharma? It cannot be considered with the heart or spoken in words. On the part of the Buddhas, it is not the slightest bit greater. On the part of living beings, it is not the slightest bit smaller. On the part of the Buddhas, it is not pure. On the part of living beings, it is not defiled. On the part of the Buddha, it is not extinguished. On the part of living beings, it is not produced. The basic substance of the wonderful dharma is neither produced nor destroyed, neither defiled nor pure, neither increased or decreased.

The wonderful dharma is inherent within everyone of us; no one lacks it. However, we do not know of it. This is called Identity with the Buddha in Principle. Speaking in terms of the principle, we are Buddhas, based on the principle that we all possess the Buddhanature. This is not to say, however, that we are Buddhas right now. In principle we are identical with the Buddha. You could say that everyone is a Buddha, but only in terms of principle, as we have not specifically realized Buddhahood yet. In principle, then, everyone has the Buddhanature and everyone is a potential Buddha. If they cultivate according to the Buddhadharma, they can realize Buddhahood.

2. Nominal Identity with the Buddha.
When we listen to lectures on the Sutras, we gain understanding of the Buddha's doctrines. We understand that the heart *(Skt. citta)* itself is the Buddha. The Buddha is just the heart. The Buddha taught the dharmas for the hearts of living beings. If living beings had no hearts, the Buddha would not have taught the Dharma. To understand that the terms "heart" and "Buddha" correspond is called Nominal Identity with the Buddha.

3. Identity with the Buddha in Contemplation and Practice.
If you merely understand that the heart is the Buddha and the Buddha is the heart and understand the Nominal Identity with the Buddha, but do not apply effort at actual cultivation, it's useless. You must cultivate. Our self-nature is the Buddhanature, and it is like gold inside a gold mine. Cultivation is like

mining the gold. Once the gold is mined out, it must still be smelted and refined until it is pure, solid gold. Identity with the Buddha in Principle is like the gold hidden in the mine. Nominal Identity with the Buddha is like the gold when it has been taken from the mine. If you cultivate and discipline yourself, that is like refining the gold and is called Identity with the Buddha in Contemplation and Practice. You have refined the gold, but you have not yet arrived at perfection.

4. *Similar Identity with the Buddha.*

If you cultivate energetically, sitting in Dhyana meditation, reciting the Buddha's name, or reciting Sutras, doing so with singleminded concentration, you will reach the level where, inwardly the six sense organs no longer exist, and, outwardly, the six sense objects have perished.

> Inwardly, no body or mind, and
> Outwardly, no world.
> One is then released
> From the organs and their objects.

At that time, there is no mark of people and even less the mark of self. There is no mark of living beings and no mark of a lifespan. There is no thought of the past, no thought of the present, and no thought of the future. The three phases of thought are completely gone and the four marks are emptied. At that time you will have obtained a bit of the flavor of the wonderful dharma. However, you do not yet know its full taste. This is called Similar Identity with the Buddha.

5. *Identity with the Buddha Through Partial Certification.*

You can't stop here, however. You must continue to cultivate with effort until, as they say in the Dhyana School, you see your original face, see what you are basically like. In the *T'ien T'ai* School this is called the attainment of the Three Truths in a Single Thought. The Three Truths are the Truth of Emptiness, the Truth of Falseness, and the Truth of the Middle Way.

In the practice of the Pure Land, it is described in *The Amitabha Sutra* as having "one heart, unconfused." You recite "Namo Amitabha Buddha," with undeviating singlemindedness until the wind will not blow against you and the rain won't fall on you. A unity is created and the entire universe is all contained within the single thought of "Namo Amitabha Buddha." At that time there are no mountains and there are no rivers, no lands, no buildings, no trees or plants, no self, no others, no living beings, and no lifespan. Everything is empty. You recite the Buddha's name until, even if you wanted

to stop reciting, you couldn't. The recitation is like
a waterfall and you can't stop it. This is called "one
heart, unconfused." It is the attainment of the Buddha-
recitation samadhi. The recitation now becomes auto-
matic. You may think, "I want to quit reciting," but
inside of you "Namo Amitabha Buddha" continues like
flowing water. I will tell you something now: This
state is so wonderful that when you hear the sound of
people talking, it sounds like they are saying, "Namo
Amitabha Buddha." The blowing wind also whispers,
"Namo Amitabha Buddha." The rushing streams recite,
"Namo Amitabha Buddha."

> The water flows, the wind blows--
> Proclaiming the Mahayana...

Everything becomes the Great Vehicle Dharma. Would
you say this state is wonderful or not? It is extremely
wonderful--"one heart, unconfused." When you arrive at
this state you will see Amitabha Buddha and the pools
made of the seven jewels. You will see the lotus flowers
of four colors--green-colored of green light, yellow
colored of yellow light, white-colored of white light,
red-colored, of red light. At that time, not only in
this world, but in a hundred worlds, you can realize
Buddhahood. You can go to any world you like and realize
Buddhahood there. In the Pure Land Dharma-door, this
is what is known as "one heart, unconfused." It's not
a matter of having a few strange experiences. People
who cultivate often meet up with strange situations.
The important thing is not to be attached to them. In
the Dhyana School they say,

> If the Buddha comes, slay the Buddha.
> If the demon comes, slay the demon.

If the Buddha arrives you should not be affected. Cultivate samadhi power. Don't think, "How delightful! The
Buddha has come!" *The Vajra Sutra* says, "Everything that
has marks is empty and false." And just what do you
think you are doing, getting so happy? *The Vajra Sutra*
also says, "If you see all marks as no-marks, just that
is to see the Thus Come One." If, in the midst of marks,
you can perceive their emptiness, that is wonderful
existence. True emptiness is basically not empty and
wonderful existence is basically not existence. Is this
wonderful or not? At that time you will have reached
the level of Identity with the Buddha Through Partial
Certification. But you have not yet reached the level
of Ultimate Identity.

   6. *Ultimate Identity with the Buddha.*

   To reach the level of Ultimate Identity with the
Buddha, you must plumb the source of the Dharma, as

Shakyamuni Buddha did one night when, sitting beneath
the Bodhi Tree, he saw a bright star and awoke to the
Way. At that time he won ultimate certification and
attainment. This is called Ultimate Identity with the
Buddha for at this time you have personally certified
to the attainment of the basic substance of the Dharma
and have truly accomplished Buddhahood.

This has been a discussion of the wonderful dharma
according to the Six Levels of Identity with the Buddha.

The state of the wonderful dharma cannot be known
through deliberation or discrimination. It is wonderful,
but few can use it.

Long ago, there was an enlightened layperson named
P'ang. After his enlightenment he thought, "I have
passed through lifetime after lifetime through limitless
aeons and only now have I become enlightened. It's a
very difficult matter, indeed. As to understanding the
wonderful dharma:
> It's hard, it's hard,
> It's really, really hard--
> Like putting seeds on the leaves
> Of trees in the yard.

The leaves grow every which way and the seeds keep
falling off! How much time would it take to cover them
with tiny sesame seeds? This is like trying to cultivate
and change one's faults. They keep popping up every day.
You try not to get angry, but something happens to test
you out, to see whether or not you will lose your temper.
You may decide to quit drinking and then who should
arrive but your old drinking buddy! You tell him, "I've
quit drinking."

"Just one for old time's sake," he says, and off you
go. Then the next day another friend shows up and asks
you out for a drink. "You went drinking with so and so,"
he says. "How can you refuse to go with me?"

It's not easy to quit drinking. It's not easy to
quit doing anything that's bad for you, in fact. It's
as hard to break those old bad habits as it is to put
a bushel of sesame seeds, one by one, neatly on the
leaves of a tree. That's what Layperson P'ang said
about the problem.

Although Layperson P'ang had a wife, he was enlightened. His wife was also enlightened and so were
his son and daughter. Hearing him comment in this way,
his enlightened wife spoke up and said, "You say it's
difficult? I don't see it that way. For me, what I
have to say about attaining the wonderful dharma is--
> It's easy, it's easy
> It's easy, as I find

> On the tip of every blade of grass
> The Patriarch's mind.

Every blade of grass, every bush and tree--they all reveal the Buddha's mind-seal Dharma and the wonderful meaning of the Patriarch from the West, Bodhidharma. Of the green bamboo and they yellow flowers, none are not Prajna. They are the manifestation of wisdom. As the Sung Dynasty poet Su Tung-p'o wrote:

> Of the colors of the mountains,
> > none are not the clear, pure body;
> Of the sounds of the streams,
> > none are not the vast, long tongue.

The mountain's colors are all the immaculate Dharmabody of the Buddha. The sound of the streams is the vast long tongue of the Buddha. As it says in *The Amitabha Sutra*, "In his own country each (Buddha) brings forth the appearance of a vast and long tongue, everywhere covering the three thousand great thousand worlds, and speaks the sincere and actual words..."

What is not wonderful dharma? Every single blade of grass is wonderful dharma. What is hard, what is difficult about it?

So the two elder P'angs held opposing views. One said it was easy, the other said it was hard. Then, their little girl, Ling-chao, happened by and offered her view on the matter:

> It's not easy; it's not hard.
> It's not easy; it's not hard.
> It's not easy; it's not hard.
> I eat when I'm hungry--
> And I sleep when I'm tired!

This shows that the wonderful dharma is within all of our daily activities. Eating, wearing clothes, sleeping--all are wonderful dharma. True cultivators eat every day and yet don't swallow a single grain. All day they wear clothes, but don't wear a single thread. Are these two statements self-contradictory? Are they lies? No. They describe a state in which the heart is not present, where one looks and yet does not see, listens and yet does not hear, eats and yet does not taste. It is the state of "no heart," in which one eats and yet does not eat, wears clothes and yet does not wear clothes, sleeps and yet does not sleep. Although one sleeps, it is the same as waking. Why? Because one is not muddled. When ordinary people sleep they have confused dreams filled with false thoughts. When enlightened people sleep, they are as clear as when they are awake.

In China, there was a National Master named Yü-lin

who was extremely intelligent. One day his teacher
announced to Yü-lin and his Dharma brother Yü-feng,
that he would pass on the Dharma to anyone who could
memorize *The Lotus Sutra* in a day and a night. Since
Yü-feng slept all day, Yü-lin figured he could surely
memorize it first and come out number one. But when he
went to his teacher and said, "I can recite it! What
about my Dharma brother?" his teacher said, "He recited it for me last night." This was because Yu-feng's
realm was like that of P'ang's little daughter. Although
he appeared to be sleeping, he was actually in samadhi.
One can enter samadhi sitting, walking, standing, or
reclining. People who don't know how to do the work
find every place to be either too noisy or too unclean.
If your heart is pure, all places are pure. So little
girl P'ang said,

> It's not easy; it's not hard.
> I eat when I'm hungry,
> And I sleep when I'm tired.

It's all a manifestation of the wonderful dharma.

The seventh consciousness is the consciousness of
deliberation. The sixth (mind) consciousness is the
consciousness of discrimination. In *The Shurangama Sutra*
the Buddha tells Ananda, "When you realize Buddhahood,
it is because of your six sense organs. If you fall
into the lower realms, it is also because of your six
sense organs." The six sense organs, plus the six sense
objects, plus the corresponding consciousnesses form the
eighteen realms. The eighteen realms are wonderful
dharma. They are manifestations of the Thus Come One's
storehouse nature. However, this applies when no
deliberation or discrimination takes place. If there is
deliberation and discrimination, one falls into the pit
of the mind consciousness.

If you tell ordinary people not to deliberate,
they will deliberate even more. If you tell them not to
discriminate, they will discriminate even more. They
are unable to turn their minds to one-pointedness. They
are unable to turn their consiousness into wisdom. Wisdom is consciousness transformed; consciousness turns
into wisdom. Wisdom is also a wonderful dharma. On the
part of living beings, wisdom has turned into consciousness. Their inherent wisdom has turned into consciousness. Thus, the wonderful has become coarse. The
Buddhas have turned consciousness into wisdom and so the
coarse has become wonderful. The coarse is unwonderful;
the wonderful is not coarse. The Buddhas have turned
consciousness into wisdom and so within the pit of the

mind consciousness they obtain genuine wisdom and certify to the attainment of the wonderful dharma.

We have said that the wonderful cannot be thought of with the heart or expressed in words. But, speaking around and around it, we still don't understand it. Although it is wonderful, we haven't understood it, and so I will tell another true story to prove the wonder of the wonderful dharma:

There was once a monk who recited *The Dharma Flower Sutra* every day. I have tried this myself, and in a single day you can just barely get through the entire seven rolls of the Sutra. As the Sutra says that the merit and virtue obtained by one who copies the Sutra out is inconceivable, the monk decided to write it out. Stroke by stroke, word by word, he reverently copied it without making a single mistake. He finished in the middle of a cold Manchurian winter. When he put his brush in the water to rinse it out, the water froze to form a lotus on the brush-tip and continued to freeze forming a larger and larger lotus. Because of this he gave himself the name "The Ice-lotus Bhikshu." Where did the ice-lotus come from? And why did it bloom so big? Many people witnessed this event. It really happened! Would you say it was a wonderful dharma?

There was another Bhikshu in China who served as an advisor to the Emperor. Everyday, when he left the monastery to go to the Court, as soon as he mounted his horse he began reciting *The Dharma Flower Sutra* from memory and by the time he arrived at the Palace, he had recited the first roll. Suddenly, one day his horse died. At the same moment, a son was born in the house of a layman who lived across from the monastery. When the child was born, his mother had an inconceivable dream. She dreamt the monk's horse came galloping up to her house and ran right into her chest. Just then she gave birth to the child. Thinking her dream very unusual, she told her relatives to go see if the horse was at the monastery. Sure enough, they discovered that the horse had just died. She knew, then, that the horse had been reborn as her son and so she sent him to the monastery right away to become a monk.

The child was outrageously stupid and no matter how the monks tried, there was no way to teach him to read or write. He couldn't read a single word and simply couldn't be taught. One day, a Bhikshu began to teach him *The Dharma Flower Sutra*, orally, word by word and he learned it right away. He learned the entire first roll in no time, but couldn't remember any of the second roll at all. Why was this? When he was a horse,

he had heard the monk recite the first roll every day
on his way to the Court and so he could remember it.
Because the horse had heard the Sutra recited every day
it got reborn as a person. It is clear that the merit
and virtue of *The Lotus Sutra* is inconceivable.

During the Chin Dynasty a similar event took place.
In Yunnan there was a person named Ch'en Tung-yüan who
believed in Kuan-yin Bodhisattva and went to P'u-t'ou
in Nan-hai, the sacred Bodhimanda of Kuan-yin Bodhisattva, to pay reverence to the Bodhisattva. After
bowing, he noticed a monk reciting *The Lotus Sutra* and
requested the monk to recite the Sutra so that his dead
mother might cross over to bliss and leave behind all
suffering. The monk did so and while he was reciting
the powerful ox in the man's home suddenly died. That
was nothing in itself, but later that night the ox came
to Ch'en Tung-yüan in a dream and said, "I am your
mother. Because I created weighty offenses through im-
proper speech I was reborn as an ox. The Dharma Master's
recitation of the Sutra has caused me to leave the body
of an ox, but, unfortunately, I am still suffering because I am now in hell. Please ask the monk to recite
the Sutra for me again."

Ch'en Tung-yüan went back to P'u-t'ou Mountain and
asked the monk to recite the Sutra again. Although the
monk was sincere in reciting the Sutra, he liked to
have a glass of wine now and then. Hearing Ch'en
Tung-yüan's request, he rose early and knelt in front
of the Buddha to recite. By the time he reached the
fourth roll, his throat was parched. There was no tea
around, but he noticed he had left his wine glass sitting full on the table. Before finishing the last three
rolls of the Sutra, he drank the wine. Ch'en Tung-yüan
again dreamt of his mother. He dreamt that she came to
him again as an ox. She said, "Son, while the first
four rolls of the Sutra were being recited, a brilliant,
golden light filled the hells and golden lotuses welled
up out of the ground. But, just as I was about to get
out, suddenly they were filled with the stink of wine
and so the last three rolls had no great effect. Please
ask the Dharma Master to recite the Sutra again."

Ch'en Tung-yüan related his dream to the monk who
realized that he was deluding himself by thinking that
his drinking was a minor offense. From then on he
strictly observed the precept against taking intoxicants
and began cultivating the Way in earnest.

From the above incidents, it is obvious that the
wonderful dharma is inconceivable and wonderful beyond
words.

Students of the Buddhadharma who hear of the wonderful advantages attained through recitation of the Sutra, that animals who hear the Sutra can be reborn as humans and that hungry ghosts dwelling in hell can be reborn in the heavens, may decide to take up recitation of the Sutra as a form of cultivation. However, be careful not to become self-satisfied and think that because you have recited the Sutra you have acquired merit. If you become arrogant, not only will you gain no merit, you will be wasting your time and will only be planting a few good roots. Cultivators must never be arrogant or haughty. They must always be courteous and humble.

In *The Sixth Patriarch's Sutra* we read about Bhikshu Fa-ta who had recited *The Dharma Flower Sutra* over three thousand times and consequently became arrogant. He went to meet the Sixth Patiarch, the Great Master Hui-neng. When those who have left the home-life meet the Abbot of a monastery, they should make obeisance very respectfully, dressed in full robes and carrying their sitting cloth. However, Fa-ta's three thousand Sutra-recitations got in his way so that when he bowed, his head didn't touch the ground. The Sixth Patriarch said, "No doubt there is something on your mind? What do you practice?"

Fa-ta was rather blunt in his reply and said proudly, "I have recited *The Dharma Flower Sutra* over three thousand times."

"Really?" said the Sixth Patriarch. "I don't care if you have recited it ten thousand times. If you understood the Sutra's meaning you would not be so arrogant." Then, he spoke a verse:

> As bowing is basically to subdue arrogance,
> Why didn't your head touch the ground?
> The mind confused, the Dharma Flower turns it;
> The enlightened mind turns the Dharma Flower.
> Reciting the Sutra so long
>   without understanding it,
> Has put you at odds with its meaning.

The Chinese word for "turn" also means "recite." When you are unclear, although you recite the Sutra, you are turned by it; if you understand, you can truly recite, that is, "turn" the Sutra. Turning the Sutra is wonderful dharma. Turning the Sutra is the wonderful aspect of the unwonderful. Being turned by the Sutra is the unwonderful aspect of the wonderful. If you have recited the Sutra three thousand times, but do not understand it, you become the Sutra's enemy. Originally, your heart and the Sutra were one, but now they are divided because you keep thinking, "I have recited the

Sutra over three thousand times; I have merit!" In this way, an obstruction is created. Not understanding the Sutra's principles, you have been unable to rid yourself of arrogance."

So no matter who you are, if you accumulate merit, do not become arrogant about it. Students of the Buddhadharma must be humble and courteous towards everyone and never be proud or arrogant. I hope that everyone will take note of this point and not just let it go in one ear and out the other.

The Lotus Flower

The concept of the wonderful dharma is extremely broad and one could never finish speaking of it. So, for now, we will move on with the discussion of the title of the Sutra and discuss the next two words: "Lotus Flower."

The lotus is a most rare flower. It blooms and bears fruit at the same time. When the lotus blooms, the lotus seeds appear. The lotus takes root in the mud and its stem grows up through the water. The flower is neither in the mud nor the water, but blooms above the surface of the water. The root in the mud represents common people. The stem in the water represents those of the Two Vehicles. Common people are attached to existence; the mud is an analogy for "existence." Those of the Two Vehicles are attached to emptiness; the stem in the water represents emptiness. The lotus flower, which blooms above the water, represents the transcendence of emptiness and existence and represents the Absolute Principle of the Middle Way in which there is neither falling into emptiness nor going to the extreme of existence. Emptiness and existence are the two "extremes." To be unattached to either of the two extremes is the Absolute Principle of the Middle Way.

Why do we say that the lotus flower represents the Absolute Principle of the Middle way, the Great Teaching, Perfect and Sudden?

We say this because the lotus flower's blooming and bearing fruit simultaneously represents the non-duality of cause and effect. As the cause is thus, thus is the effect. If the cause planted is one of Buddhahood, the effect will be one of Buddhahood.

The lotus blooming and bearing fruit simultaneously also represents the "opening of the provisional to manifest the real." The blooming of the lotus represents the "opening" of the provisional dharma. The lotus

seeds which are revealed when the lotus blooms represent
the real Dharma. Provisional Dharma refers to expedient
devices and real Dharma is the genuine, "not-false"
Dharma, the Principle of the Real Mark.

Why did the Buddha appear in the world? It was for
the sake of teaching all living beings to become enlightened. The Buddha appeared in the world because of the
problem of living beings' birth and death. So the
Sutra says, "The Buddha appeared in the world for the
reason of the one Great Matter." The Great Matter is
the problem of living beings' birth and death.

"But," someone might object, "everyone is born and
dies; birth and death is the most democratic event in
heaven and earth. Why make such an issue of it?"

That's a good question. However, although everyone is born and dies--birth, death, death and rebirth,
death and rebirth again--ultimately, what use is it?
Ultimately what advantage does it have? Chuang-tzu spoke
with sound principle when he said,

> "My life has a limit, but knowledge
> is unlimited. To pursue the unlimited
> with that which is limited is dangerous
> indeed!"

He said, "My life has a limit, but knowledge has no end.
To study endless knowledge with one's finite life is
futile. It cannot be done."

However, Chuang-tzu only knew half the story. He
didn't see the full picture. He knew that life has an
end, but he didn't know that, when it is over, there is
rebirth and another beginning. When one life ends,
another begins. This is like previously the toll
collectors on the Golden Gate Bridge used to collect
from the cars as they came and went. Only later did
they realize that anyone who left the City was likely
to return and that they could save time and energy by
simply doubling the toll and collecting only from in-
coming traffic. Chuang-tzu understood the road out, but
not the road back.

Human life is a round-trip affair. When you leave
you always return. If you understand how you were born,
you will be able to understand the problem of death.
If you do not understand how you were born, you will not
understand the problem of death. Coming, you will be
muddled; going you will be muddled. Coming, you will
not understand; going you will not understand. In *The
Confucian Analects*, we read,

> "Tzu-lu asked about how to serve ghosts
> and spirits. The Master said, 'Until
> you know how to serve people, how can

you serve ghosts?' Tzu-lu then dared
to ask a question about the dead and
the Master replied, 'Until you know
about the living, how can you know
about the dead?'"
    Tzu-lu said, "I realize I'm being rather bold, but
may I ask about the method for dying? What is the
flavor of death? What is it like?" Actually Tzu-lu was
just trying to make trouble. Confucius hadn't died yet,
why ask him about death? No doubt Confucius was rather
old and certainly afraid of death and so he said, "If
you don't know how to live, how can you know how to die?"
Confucius lived to be very old, but this proves that he
was afraid of death and still retained the "mark of a
lifespan." What he meant by his answer was, "However
you were born, that is how you will die."
    Then you ask, "How are we born?"
    Now we will get down to the basic problem and
everyone should pay close attention. People are born
because of emotion and sexual desire and they die because of emotion and sexual desire. If you have no
emotion or sexual desire then you do not undergo birth
or death. Therefore, the problem of birth and death
arises because of thoughts of sexual desire. If you
sever thoughts of sexual desire you will then end birth
and death. However, Tzu-lu didn't understand the problem
and Confucius didn't answer him in terms of the problem;
he just skirted the issue. But I will tell all of you
now that birth and death is a very important problem.
The Buddha appeared in the world simply because of the
problem of living beings' birth and death.

"You Can't Take it With You"

    Once there was a fabulously wealthy old man who had
a beautiful wife and three fine, intelligent sons. But,
from the time this man was born, he didn't pay any
attention to anything but money. He ignored his father,
his mother, and his brothers and sisters. The only
thing he didn't ignore was money. He knew money like
the back of his hand. It was his best friend and
closest relative. He even wrote a verse about it:
        "What heaven has conferred is called
        'Money. According to this money it is
        called 'money.' Money...ahh...may not
        be left for a moment."
Actually, this is a rather perverted take-off on the
first chapter of the Chinese classic, *The Doctrine of the
Mean,* which reads, "That which has been conferred by

heaven is called the nature; according with the nature
is called the path...The path may not be left for
a moment."

He named his oldest son "Gold." His second son
he named "Silver." He decided to give his third son
an unusual name, and called him, "Karmic Obstacle."
When this third son had grown up and he was old, he got
sick. He was completely bed-ridden and couldn't walk.
Although he was very rich, after he had been sick for
some time, no one looked after him. His beautiful wife
kept her distance and his intelligent sons never came to
visit him. He gritted his teeth and thought, "I hope I
hurry up and die. But being dead alone in King Yama's
den will be very lonely. I should take someone with
me." He called for his wife and said, "I'm not going
to recover from this lingering illness. I hope to die
soon. Won't you go with me?"

"How can you ask a thing like that?" she said.
"Nobody can die for anyone else. How could you expect
me to want to go along with you? Are you sure you
haven't lost your marbles?"

So the old man called his eldest son. "Gold," he
said. "I have always loved you the most. Did you know
that?"

"Yes, Father," said his son. "I know you love me
the most."

"Well, Son, now I'm going to die. Would you go
along with me?"

"You old blockhead!" came the reply. "You're an
old man. I'm young. How can you ask me to do something
like that? And you claim to be fond of me? If you were,
you wouldn't ask me to die with you!" and he ran off.

Then the old man spoke to his second son, "Silver,
won't you die with me?"

"You're really messed up," said his son. "How can
you expect me to die just because you are dying?"

There was nothing the man could do but call for his
youngest son, Karmic Obstacle. "You are the youngest,"
he said. "I love you the most. I could die, but I can't
bear to part with you. What am I going to do?" He
didn't dare ask outright for his son to go with him, but
the boy caught on right away.

"If you love me so much, I'll go with you," said
his son. The old man was delighted.

"You haven't let me down," he said. "I always liked
you best and now I know you are my most filial son."

So his pretty wife wouldn't go with him and his sons
Gold and Silver wouldn't go. The only one who went with
his father to hell was his young son Karmic Obstacle. So

it is said,

> You can't take your Gold and Silver
> With you on your dying day;
> But your karmic obstacles
> Stick with you all the way!
> To be born in the Blissful Land
> Merely recite Amitabha's name.

Just recite, "Namo Amitabha Buddha" to be reborn in the Land of Ultimate Bliss, and be free of the suffering of the turning wheel of rebirth. Besides, if you want to get rich, the Land of Ultimate Bliss is covered with gold. No paupers are there. If the old man had woken up and recited "Namo Amitabha Buddha" he could have taken his sons Gold and Silver with him and he wouldn't have been so lonely.

This story should serve to warn us to use every last bit of strength we have to do good deeds. Don't wait until you have no strength, until your dying breath, because then it will be too late. On the basis of the good roots we have planted in former lives, we should nurture our blessings and wisdom in this present life.

There are many different kinds of flowers. Some flowers bloom but bear no fruit. They are like people who talk big, but don't act on their words. They may say they are going to build a Buddha image, for example, but they never do it. This is called a sterile bloom. Such barren flowers represent non-Buddhist religions which appear to be very popular. They cultivate pure conduct and various types of asceticism, but they bear no fruit, no accomplishment. They are like the flowers which bear no fruit.

Other flowers bear many fruits from a single bloom. This represents common people who practice many kinds of filial conduct. By serving and making offerings to their parents, teachers, and elders, they create much merit, and in the future they will be reborn among people as noble, wealthy folk. This is called "one flower with many fruits." Other flowers have many flowers but only one fruit. This represents the Vehicle of the Sound Hearers who cultivate many types of asceticism, but obtain only the "Nirvana with residue." This is called "many flowers, but one fruit."

Other flowers have one bloom and one fruit. This represents the Condition-enlightened Ones. They practice living in solitude, deep in the mountains, away from the bustle of human life. Through their cultivation of this one practice, they obtain the position of Condition-enlightened Ones.

Other flowers may be said to first bear fruit and then bloom. This represents those who have obtained the first fruit of Arhatship, the Stream-winners, who still have cultivation ahead of them. Some flowers first bloom and then bear fruit. This represents the Bodhisattva Vehicle. The Bodhisattvas first cultivate and then obtain the position of Bodhisattvahood.

However, the various flowers listed above cannot be used when speaking of the wonderful dharma. Only the lotus can be used as an analogy for the wonderful dharma because it blooms and bears fruit at the same time; this represents the identity of the real and the provisional. The bloom represents the provisional Dharma and the fruit represents the real Dharma. However, the provisional Dharma is just the real Dharma. It is said, "The provisional manifests for the sake of the real." Why does the flower bloom? For the sake of the fruit. Thus, the Buddha spoke the Agama, Vaipulya, and Prajna Sutras in preparation for speaking *The Dharma Flower Sutra*. The Dharmas taught prior to this were provisional not real. In the Dharma Flower Assembly, the real Dharma was taught, the real teaching, the "provisional was opened to manifest the real." The preceding teachings were dispensed with and the real Dharma was made manifest. This is what is meant by "the flower blooms and the seeds appear." As soon as the flower blooms, the lotus seeds appear. This represents the "opening of the provisional to manifest the actual."

When the lotus petals fall away, the seedpod stands alone. This represents "annulling the provisional to establish the real," abandoning the provisional Dharma and retaining the real Dharma.

There are also the two gates: the root and and branches. By way of analogy, the moon in empty space could be called the "root" and the moon's reflection in the waters, the branches. Although there is only one root, there are countless branches. The branches grow from the root. When the branches are pushed aside, the root is manifest. The doctrine here is the same as that of "bestowing the provisional for the sake of the real; opening the provisional to reveal the real; annulling the provisional to establish the real."

Within the Sutra the root gate refers to the Sutra text before the point where the sixteen princes decide to leave home which was a long, long time ago. Shakyamuni Buddha's recent appearance in the world is called the "branches gate." He manifested in the body of a Buddha to teach the Dharma to living beings. Actually, Shakyamuni Buddha did not realize Buddhahood in this

Saha world some three thousand years ago. He realized
Buddhahood many long aeons ago. So, in *The Brahma Net
Sutra* he says, "I have come to this Saha world eight
thousand times." The Saha world we currently live in
is a relatively young world. There have been old Saha
worlds and prior Saha worlds which are called "roots."
The present Saha world is one of the "branches." The
Buddhadharma is infinite and endless. The knowledge and
vision, the scope of perception of living beings, cannot
fathom or reckon it. It is therefore called a wonderful
dharma.

In general, the lotus represents the wonderful
dharma. The lotus flower is just the wonderful dharma;
the wonderful dharma is just the lotus flower. This is
the analogy of the Sutra.

All Sutras have a specific title and a common title.
The Wonderful Dharma Lotus Flower is the specific title of
the Sutra. The word *Sutra* is the common title, because
all discourses spoken by the Buddha are called Sutras,
just like all people are called "people." We are all
people and have that title in common. Specifically,
each person has his own particular name, and so do the
Sutras.

Sutra

Sutra is a Sanskrit word interpreted as meaning
"a tallying text." Above, a Sutra tallies with the wonderful principles of all Buddhas and below it tallies
with the opportunities for teaching living beings. The
word Sutra can also be interpreted in many other ways:

1. A road. A Sutra is a road which one may travel
from the status of a common person to the position of
Buddhahood.

2. Basic Dharma. The Sutras are the roots, the
foundation of the Dharma.

3. Manifestation. The Sutras clearly instruct and
reveal to us the principles of the Buddhadharma.

4. A Bubbling spring. The principles flow from the
Sutras like water gushing ceaselessly from the earth.

5. A guideline. To make guidelines, ancient
carpenters and stone masons used a string covered with
black ink. They held the string taught, pulled it up,
and let it snap to make a straight, black line. Sutras
set forth guidelines and rules for cultivation. "Without a compass and T-square," it is said, "you can't draw
circles and squares." Without the guidance of the
Sutras, you cannot cultivate the Way.

6. A flower garland. The principles are linked to-

gether in the Sutras like flowers woven into a garland.
The word Sutra also has four additional meanings:
1. Stringing together. The Sutras string together
the doctrines of the Dharma from beginning to end in an
orderly fashion.
2. Attracting.Living beings all have their own
particular tastes. Sour, hot, salty, or sweet--whatever
your taste, the Sutras contain them all. You can find
whichever Dharma-door you like in the Sutras. If you
like to investigate Dhyana, the doctrines of meditation
are discussed in the Sutras. If you like to study the
teachings, to lecture on the Sutras and speak the
Dharma, you can study how to do so in the Sutras. For
example, you will learn that when you explain the Sutras
you discuss the Seven Sutra Title Classifications and
the Five Profound Meanings. If you like to study the
Vinaya and specialize in holding the precepts, you can
also study them in the texts. If you like to recite
mantras and practice the Secret School dharmas, you can
learn about them in the Sutras. All the various Dharma-
doors are found in the Sutras and, according to your
disposition, you may cultivate whichever one suits you.
Thus, the Sutras attract beings according to their
potentials and dispositions.
3. Permananent. From the time the Buddha spoke the
Sutras up until the present, the Buddha's Sutras have not
been changed. Not one word can be added to them and not
one word can be omitted.
4. A method. The methods set forth for cultivation
in the Sutras are those taught by the Buddhas of the
past, present, and future. Living beings of the past,
present, and future cultivate according to them.
As previously mentioned, the Sanskrit word Sutra
is interpreted as a "tallying text." Above, it tallies
with the heart of the Buddhas and below with the hearts
of living beings. The heart, the Buddha, and living
beings are not separate. The heart-dharma, the living
beings dharma, and the Buddhadharma ultimately are the
same.
The word Sutra has many other meanings which will
not be discussed here. This has been a general discussion of the first of the Five Profound Meanings,
that is, Explaining the Title.
Great Master *Chih-che* discussed the single word
"wonderful" for ninety days. But really, you couldn't
finish in nine hundred, or nine thousand, or for that
matter, ninety thousand days. Why? Because it's
wonderful. What is wonderful can never be fully expressed
in speech. Even if you were to explain it for several

great aeons, it would be hard to finish. So for now, we will merely present this general discussion of the title of *The Wonderful Dharma Lotus Flower Sutra*.

Discrimination of the Substance:

The second of the Five Profound Meanings is the Discrimination of the Substance. If we don't know the substance of the Sutra, how can we expect to be able to understand its principles? This Sutra takes the Real Mark as its substance. The Real Mark is unmarked and yet there is nothing it does not mark. All marks are produced from the Real Mark. Not only do all marks come from the Real Mark, but all the Buddhas and Bodhisattvas, Sound Hearers and Condition-enlightened Ones come from the Real Mark as well. And who created the Real Mark? No one. It was originally there. How did it get there? It was just *there*, that's all. Why ask such a question? The Real Mark preceded all the Buddhas and Bodhisattvas and is the mother of all things--all creation is born from the Real Mark.

The Wonderful Dharma Lotus Flower Sutra takes the Real Mark as its substance and so all the Buddhas, Bodhisattvas, Sound Hearers, Condition-enlightened Ones, and all living beings are born from this Sutra. But we have been away too long. We have forgotten our original home, we have forgotten our original mother and so we find the Sutra very new. Having the chance to hear a lecture on this Sutra is like finding the road which will take us back home. Thus, the Sutra takes the Real Mark as its substance.

Clarification of the Doctrine:

The third of the Five Profound Meanings is to Clarify the Doctrine. This Sutra takes the cause and effect of the One Vehicle as its doctrine. As the text says, "There is only the One Buddha Vehicle. There are no other vehicles." Previously, the Buddha had spoken of the Three Vehicles--the Bodhisattva Vehicle, the Sound Hearer Vehicle, and the Condition-enlightened Vehicle. He also taught the Five Vehicles which are those three plus the Vehicle of People and the Vehicle of Gods. But in this Sutra the Five Vehicles are dispensed with and only the One Vehicle, the Supreme Vehicle, the Buddha Vehicle, is expounded. So the doctrine of the Sutra is the cause and effect of the One Vehicle.

Why is the lotus flower used as an analogy? Because the lotus blooms and bears fruit at the same time. This represents the identity of cause and effect. The cause is the cause of Buddhahood and the effect is the position of Buddhahood. Thus, the Sutra takes the cause and effect of the One Vehicle as its doctrine.

Discussion of the Function

The fourth of the Five Profound Meanings is to Discuss the Function. What is the function of this Sutra? The function of the Sutra is to sever doubts and awaken faith. While reciting *The Dharma Flower Sutra*, Great Master *Chih-che* became enlightened and obtained the Dharani of a Single Revolution. On the basis of that enlightenment, he systematized the *T'ien T'ai* School. So do not consider this Sutra a simple one. All the Buddhas, Bodhisattvas, and Patriarchs are born from *The Dharma Flower Sutra*.

Determination of the Teaching Mark

The fifth of the Five Profound Meanings is to Determine the Teaching Mark. The Teaching Mark of this Sutra is clarified butter. As previously mentioned, the Five Periods of the Buddha's teaching are represented by an analogy to milk products. The Avatamsaka Period may be compared to whole milk. The Agama Period is compared to coagulated milk. The Vaipulya Period is like curdled milk. The Prajna Period is like butter. The Lotus-Nirvana Period is like clarified butter. It has a subtle, wonderful taste. Just talking about it makes one's mouth water. But don't worry; now that I am lecturing on the Sutra, you will taste this wonderful flavor, and you will know how fine it really is. Thus, the Teaching Mark of the Sutra is clarified butter.

This has been a general explanation of the Five Profound Meanings.

PART III.
The Translator

Sutra:

TRANSLATED BY TRIPITAKA MASTER KUMARAJIVA OF YAO CH'IN.

Commentary:

TRIPITAKA MASTER KUMARAJIVA (344-413 AD) translated the Sutra from Sanskrit into Chinese. His father's name was Kumarayana. Kumarayana was the son of a high official in India and, although he was heir to his father's position, he renounced the world instead and travelled everywhere in search of a good knowing advisor. Since Kumarayana's father was a high official, he was welcomed warmly wherever he went. In his travels he went to Kucha where the King, hearing that Kumarayana had set aside worldly glory, much admired him, met him at the border, and escorted him into the country. He also conferred upon him the title of National Master.

The King had a little sister named Jiva who was just

twenty years old. From birth she was so intelligent that
she looked down on all the men in her own country. The
King invited Kumarayana to a banquet and the moment Jiva
saw him she fell in love with him and wished to marry
him. Although she didn't say anything, her brother, who
was also quite intelligent, noticed her reaction. He
decided it was meant to be, and ordered Kumarayana to
marry her.

Before long, she became pregnant, and a lot of
strange things began to happen. She often visited
Ch'iao Li Ta Temple where she listened to the virtuous
masters expound upon the Dharma. Originally, she did
not understand the Indian languages, but strangely
enough   when she was pregnant with Kumarajiva, one
day while attending a feast offered to the Sangha, she
suddenly understood the Indian speakers and was able to
converse with them as well. Not only that, her eloquence
was unobstructed and her wisdom increased greatly. Everyone expressed their amazement. At that time, an Arhat
said, "The child in that woman's womb is no ordinary
child   but one of great wisdom. This is like the
situation when Shariputra was in his mother's womb.
So the child is probably just like Shariputra, the
wisest of the Buddha's Sound Hearer Disciples." When he
was still in his mother's womb, then, Kumarajiva helped
his mother become wise.

Not long after that, she expressed the desire to
leave the home-life, but her husband would not give his
consent. Two or three years later she gave birth to a
second son. Because her basic disposition was extremely
fine, when she heard the Dharma Masters expound the
Dharma, saying that everything in the world was bound up
in suffering, emptiness, and impermanence, and was
without a self, she resolved to leave home, no matter
what. At this time Kumarajiva was only seven years old.
Although his father had formerly wanted to leave home,
after his marriage to Jiva, he gave up the idea. He was
now too much in love with his beautiful wife and too
fond of his money and his position. In *The Sutra of
Forty-two Sections* it says, "It is hard to practice giving
when one is poor; it is hard to study the Way when one
is rich." Because of his wealth and rank, Kumarayana
had become confused. Not only did he not want to leave
home, he wouldn't allow his wife to leave home either.

One day, when Jiva was stolling outside the city,
she came upon a charnel field. Seeing the dry, brittle
bones scattered in great disorderly heaps, she profoundly grasped the universal truth of suffering and accordingly made a vow: "You say you won't let me leave home,"

she said, "but I'll die before I'll remain here," and
she began to fast. At first, Kumarayana didn't think
much of her not eating. But when she hadn't taken any
food, or even a drink of water, for six days, he grew
concerned. On the evening of the sixth day, seeing her
weakened condition and fearing that she might really
starve to death, he finally relented. "All right," he
said, "you may leave home. Now *please* eat something!"

Jiva replied, "First ask the Dharma Master to
cut my hair and then I will eat. Otherwise, after I
eat you might go back on your word."

Kumarayana had no choice but to go to Ch'iao Li Ta
Temple and ask the Abbot to shave his wife's head.
After that, she ate. From that time on, she studied
the Buddhadharma with great sincerity. In studying the
Dharma, sincerity is essential. Without a sincere
heart, no matter how long you study, you'll obtain nothing. Because she was so sincere--ready to starve to
death in order to leave home--and because she saw cultivation as more important than life itself, she was
able to reach the extreme of singlemindedness. She
put absolutely everything else aside and at that time
her spiritual light blazed forth and she realized the
first fruit of Arhatship.

Often she would take Kumarajiva with her to the
Temple. He was only seven years old at the time and
when he saw people bowing to the Buddha, he would do
the same. When he saw people lighting incense, he
would imitate them. Soon, he left home with his mother.
What do you think his father did? He was very upset. He
found it as hard to let go of his son as it had been to
let go of his wife. He may have wept bitter tears; it's
not known for sure. However, Kumarjiva's mother was
very firm. "Cry all you like," she said, "but we are
leaving home," and off they went.

After Kumarajiva left home, he studied the Small
Vehicle teachings and recited the Sutras at the rate of
a thousand verses of thirty-two words each per day or
32,000 words a day. That's about thirty times as many
words as there are in the Shurangama Mantra. Think it
over: Kumarajiva at seven years old could memorize that
many words in a single day. How does our intelligence
compare with his? Every day you are given twenty-four
Chinese characters to learn, but today you don't remember yesterday's lesson. How can we possibly compare
with him?

His mother soon had an awakening. Being the little
sister of a King, after she left home she was showered
with offerings. Not wishing to live in luxury and in-

tent on cultivating the Way, she decided to take Kumarajiva with her and travel about. When Kumarajiva was
nine years old, she took him to Kashmir where he studied
the Small Vehicle under the High Master Bandhudatta.
Kumarajiva worked extremely hard at his studies.
From dawn until noon, he wrote the verses out, and from
noon until the sun went down he recited them from memory.
     In addition to being intelligent, Kumarajiva was
also not lazy. Because he was intelligent, he learned
the Sutras very fast; because he was not lazy, his
learning was extensive. If he had been intelligent,
but lazy, he never would have learned very much. If
he had been industrious, but not intelligent, he also
would not have learned very much. But since he was
both, he learned very fast.
     When he was twelve he and his mother set out to
return to Kucha. As they passed through the northern
mountains of Kusana, an Arhat saw Kumarajiva and said,
"You should take good care of this little novice. If
by the time he is thirty-five he has not broken the
precepts, he will be able to cause the Buddhadharma to
flourish greatly and will save countless beings, as
did the Fourth Patriarch Upagupta in India. If his
precepts are not held intact, this will not be possible."
The Fourth Patriarch lived in a stone cave. Everytime
he converted someone, he would put a slip of bamboo in
his cave. Eventually, the cave was entirely filled
with bamboo slips, which proves that he saved hundreds
of thousands of people.
     On their way back to Kucha, they stopped in
Kashgar. There, in a temple Kumarajiva saw a large
incense burner in front of the Buddha image. It must
have weighed at least a hundred pounds. But he picked
it right up and put it over his head with no effort at
all. Once he had done this, he thought, "I'm just a
little child. How can I lift such a heavy thing?"
With that one thought, the burner suddenly became very
heavy and crashed to the ground. When his mother asked
him what was going on, he said, "The burner seemed
light and then heavy only because of discriminations
in your son's mind." Thus, he awoke to the fact that
everything is made from the mind alone. Before he had
discriminated, he lifted the burner easily. Once he
gave rise to discrimination, what had not been heavy
became heavy. From this he knew that the ten thousand
dharmas arise only from the mind.
     He remained in Kashgar studying Abhidharma texts
and was introduced to the Great Vehicle and realized
that, while the Small Vehicle was wonderful, the Great

Vehicle was the wonderful within the wonderful. He sighed and said, "In my previous study of the Small Vehicle, I was like one who did not recognize gold and took ordinary rock as something wonderful." Although the King of Kashgar was anxious to keep him in his court, the King of Kucha sent a messenger asking him to return and so Kumarajiva and his mother once again set out for Kucha.

In a small country north of Kucha, there was a master of debate who loudly beat the palace drum and announced that if anyone could beat him in a debate, he would chop off his own head and present it to that person as a gift. This, too, was similar to the incident which took place between Shariputra's uncle and the Buddha. As Kumarajiva happened to be passing through, he questioned the man about two principles which rendered him completely speechless. Since he couldn't bear to cut off his head, he bowed to Kumarajiva as his teacher and studied with him. Kumarajiva once again set out for Kucha and was welcomed at the border by the King himself.

At the age of twenty, Kumarajiva received the full precepts, that is, complete ordination, at the palace. He studied the Sarvastivadin *Vinaya in Ten Sections* under Vimalaksha, the well-known Shramana from Kashmir who had ventured to Kucha and was a renowned master of the Vinaya.

Meanwhile, Kumarajiva's mother decided to travel to India where she was to certify to the third fruit of Arhatship. Before leaving, she took a look at the causes and conditions and saw that her son's affinities lay in China. She told him, "The profound Vaipulya Teachings should be propagated extensively in China. You are the only one with the power to do this. However it will be most unbeneficial for you personally. I don't know how you feel about this..."

Kumarajiva replied, "The way of the Bodhisattva is to benefit others and forget oneself. If I can transmit the great teaching and enlighten the people I would not resent being boiled in a cauldron."

Kumarajiva remained in Kucha for two years studying the Great Vehicle Sutras. Then his uncle, the King, had a golden lion throne made for him and asked him to ascend it and speak the Dharma. But at that time Kumarajiva had something else on his mind. He wanted to convert his Small Vehicle Master, Bandhudatta. His Small Vehicle Master had a lot of disciples, and if Kumarajiva could convert him, he would convert many others as well. So, although his uncle had made him a lion throne, he

still intended to leave Kucha. This greatly upset his
uncle. "I have been so gracious as to make you this
throne," he said, "and you show me no consideration
whatever."
     Curiously enough, shortly thereafter, Bandhudatta
arrived at the border, seeking entrance into Kucha. When
border officials informed the palace, both Kumarajiva
and the King went to meet him. The King asked Bandhudatta, "Why have you come from so far?"
     Bandhudatta replied,"I came first of all because
I heard of the great awakening of my disciple, and
secondly because I heard, Great King, of your vast
propagation of the Buddha Way and I wished to meet you."
     Kumarajiva was delighted to see his teacher and
spoke for him *The Sutra of the Questions of the Virtuous
Woman*, a Great Vehicle Sutra. When he had finished,
his teacher said, "Just what particular advantages
does the Great Vehicle have that have caused you to
take it up in lieu of the Small Vehicle?"
     Kumarajiva replied, "The Great Vehicle propounds
the doctrine that dharmas are empty. The Small Vehicle
relies upon names and marks."
     Bandhudatta replied, "The Great Vehicle talks about
emptiness, but emptiness is just emptiness--nothing at
all. What's the use of studying it? If everything is
empty, then why study it?"
     Kumarajiva said, "In emptiness there is existence.
In True Emptiness there is Wonderful Existence. Within
Wonderful Existence there is True Emptiness. The Great
Vehicle is the ultimate teaching. It is not like the
Small Vehicle which restricts itself with names and
terms and does not teach genuine liberation. The Small
Vehicle is too rigid and stuffy."
     Then Bandhudatta countered, "I have an analogy for
the emptiness of the Great Vehicle. Once there was a
madman who asked a weaver to weave him a piece of fine
silk. The first piece the weaver brought him was not
fine enough, and the second was still too coarse. He
kept sending the weaver back to his loom until, in
exasperation the weaver finally confronted him with nothing at all, just his empty fist clenched in space
and said, 'Here it is. This is my finest work!'
     "'But there's nothing there,' the madman said.
     "'This silk is so fine,' said the weaver, 'that even
I, the master weaver, cannot see it. It's so fine it's
invisible.'
     "The madman was delighted and paid a handsome price
for the silk.   The other weavers also took up this

method and they all cheated the madman who paid out a
lot of money for nothing at all. Your exposition of the
Great Vehicle Dharma is exactly like that," said Bandhudatta. "You talk about emptiness and say that within
emptiness there is existence, but no one can see it."

"No, no, no," said Kumarajiva, and he continued
to explain many subtle Great Vehicle Doctrines to him
until finally, after over a month of discussion, he
won his teacher over to the Great Vehicle, and brought
him to a true understanding of the doctrine of True
Emptiness and Wonderful Existence. Then what do you
think happened?

Bandhudatta said, "I want to bow to you as my
Master."

Kumarajiva said, "You can't do that. I have already
bowed to you as my Master. How can you bow to me as your
Master?"

Bandhudatta said, "I am your Small Vehicle Master;
you can be my Great Vehicle Master. That way, we'll
both have our masters and we'll both have our vehicles
and everyone will be satisfied. It's no big problem."

In this way, Kumarajiva received his own teacher
as a disciple. It's obvious from this that the ancients
did not have a mark of self. They had true understanding. Otherwise, Bandhudatta would not have been able
to bow to his own disciple as a teacher. He would simply
have said, "I don't care how lofty your eloquence; you
are my disciple and that's that." The ancients had no
view of self. They took the Way as their teacher. All
that was necessary was for someone else to have more
virtue than they, and they would bow to them as their
teacher. They had no obstructive thoughts of rank or
position, and they were not self-centered.

One time, when the weather was extremely dry in
Kucha, and it hadn't rained for a long time, Kumarajiva
manifested great spiritual powers and set up a Dharma
Altar to seek rain. He announced, "Within three days
there will certainly be rain." Sure enough, before
three days had passed, it rained. Everyone believed in
him even more.

All the nations stood in awe of Kumarajiva and the
Kings would kneel beneath his speaking platform to
listen to him expound upon the Sutras. They would even
allow themselves to be used as chairs! Kumarajiva
would deliver lectures sitting on the backs of the Kings
who did this to show how much they honored him and how
much they esteemed the Buddhadharma.

YAO CH'IN in the name of the reign period of
Emperor Yao Hsing. Earlier, Fu Chien had set up the

Fu Ch'in Dynasty. When Fu Chien was murdered by Yao
Ch'ang, the dynasty name was changed to Yao Ch'in.
Later, when Yao Ch'ang died, Yao Hsing took the throne.

In Ch'ang An, Fu Chien's court astrologer, Ch'ih
T'ien Chien, had seen a "wisdom star" shining over
India and told Fu Chien, "In India there is a person of
great wisdom who shall be coming here to protect our
country."

Fu Chien said, "It is most likely Kumarajiva. We
should send out troops to escort him here. He then
sent General Lü Kuang with seventy thousand mounted
troops to Kucha after Kumarajiva.

Before Lü Kuang arrived in Kucha, Kumarajiva had
told the King, "China is sending troops to our country,
but they do not wish to take our land. They have
another objective and you should listen to them and
agree to their demands." But the King refused to
listen and when Lü Kuang arrived he sent out his troops
to fight. The Chinese army was large and powerful, and
Kucha was just a little country. The King was murdered
and his troops defeated.

As the King had been an ardent believer in
Buddhism, you may wonder why he was murdered. It was
because the killing karma he had created in past lives
was too heavy. It was a fixed, unavoidable retribution.

Lu Kuang captured Kumarajiva and started back. One
night he camped in a gorge at the base of two mountains.
Kumarajiva advised him not to camp there as it was an
inauspicious site, but Lü Kuang said, "What do you, a
left-home person, know about military matters?" In the
middle of the night a flood swept down the gorge and Lü
Kuang lost several thousand men. The next day he
realized that Kumarajiva was rather extraordinary, that
he had spiritual powers. Before the troops had drowned
he did not believe in him, but now he certainly did!

When Lü Kuang arrived in Ku Tsang, he heard that in
China Fu Chien had been murdered by Yao Ch'ang, who
had set up the Yao Ch'in Dynasty. Uncertain as to how
he would be received in China, Lü Kuang decided to remain in Ku Tsang and maintain his neutrality.

When Lü Kuang's most esteemed minister, Ch'ang Chih,
fell ill, a Brahman healer thought to swindle Lü Kuang
and claimed that he could cure Ch'ang Chih's illness.
Lü Kuang gave him a large sum of money, but Kumarajiva
knew the man was a swindler and said to Lü Kuang, "No
matter how much money you give him, you won't be able
to cure Ch'ang Chih's illness. I will prove it to you.
Here is a five-colored thread which I shall burn into
ashes. Then I will put the ashes in some water. If the

ashes turn back into a five-colored thread, then Ch'ang Chih's illness will not be cured. If they do not, he will get well. If you don't believe me, we'll try it out. He burned the thread and put the ashes in a cup of water. As soon as he did this, the ashes turned into a five-colored thread. Seeing this, Lü Kuang knew that Ch'ang Chih could not be cured. Soon after, Ch'ang Chih died. Lü Kuang had spent a lot of money and got no results whatsoever. This was the inconceivable state of Kumarajiva. His spiritual powers were something which ordinary people could never fathom.

In China, when Yao Ch'ang died, his son, Yao Hsing, took the throne. A loyal supporter of the Buddhadharma, he sent men to Ku Tsang to bring Kumarajiva to China. In Ku Tsang, Lü Kuang had died, and his son Lu Shao took the throne. Shortly after, Lü Tsuan, the son of one of his father's concubines, murdered Lü Shao and seized power. During the second year of Lü Tsuan's reign, a three-headed pig was born. Then a dragon was seen crawling out of a well on the outskirts of the eastern part of the city. It coiled up in front of the palace hall and remained there until dawn when it disappeared. Thinking this an auspicious portent, Lü Tsuan renamed the palace "Hovering Dragon." Then a black dragon was seen outside the throne-room gates. Lü Tsuan changed the name from "Nine Chamber Gates" to "Rising Dragon Gates."

Kumarajiva told Lü Tsuan, "The appearance of these dragons is highly inauspicious. They are *yin* dragons and their frequent appearance fortells calamities for the nation. I advise the cultivation of virtue to forestall these impending disasters."

Lü Tsuan would not hear of this. While playing chess with Kumarajiva, Lü Tsuan was about to take one of Kumarajiva's men and said, in reference to the chess more, "I cut off the Hu Nu's (barbarian's) head."

Startled, Kumarajiva said, "You cannot cut off the Hu Nu's head. The Hu Nu will cut off someone else's head." This was a prophecy, although Lü Tsuan failed to understand it as such. Lü Kuang's little brother, Lü Pao, had a son named Lü Ch'ao whose nickname was Hu Nu. At that time, Lü Ch'ao was plotting Lü Tsuan's murder. Later Lü Ch'ao did, in fact, kill Lü Tsuan, and set his older brother, Lü Lung, on the throne. It was Lü Lung who was ruling the country when Yao Hsing's troops arrived from China to take Kumarajiva.

Kumarajiva arrived in China, at Ch'ang An, in 401 A.D. and was made a National Master. He headed a translation center with over eight hundred Sangha and lay

scholars assisting him in his work. By the time he
died, he had produced over three hundred rolls of
translation.

We have proof that Kumarajiva's translations are
extremely accurate. When he was about to die, he asked
to be cremated and said, "I have translated many Sutras
during my lifetime and I personally do not know if they
are correct. If they are, when I am cremated, my
tongue will not burn. If there are mistakes, however,
it will. When his body was burned, his tongue was
found unburned in the ashes.

During the T'ang Dynasty, Vinaya Master Tao Hsüan
once asked the god Lü Hsüan Ch'ang, "Why does everyone
prefer to read Kumarajiva's translations?"

The god replied, "Kumarajiva has been the
translation master for the past seven Buddhas and so
his translations are extremely accurate.

Kumarajiva was a TRIPITAKA MASTER, one who has
mastered the Three Divisions of the Buddhist Canon:
the Sutras, Shastras, and Vinaya. A Dharma MASTER
takes the Dharma as his master and bestows the Dharma
upon others. Some Dharma Masters chant Sutras, others
maintain them in their minds and practice them with
their bodies; others write them out and still others
explain them to others.

The Dharma Master here referred to is Kumarajiva.
This Sanskrit word means "youth and long life." One
could say, "Young Kumarajiva will certainly live to a
great age. One could also say, "He is young in years,
but mature in wisdom, eloquence, and virtue. He has the
wisdom of an old man, and so he is called 'the youth
of long life.'"

It was Kumarajiva, then, the youth with the
wisdom and virtuous conduct of an elder, who translated
from Sanskrit into Chinese *The Wonderful Dharma Lotus
Flower Sutra*.

THE BUDDHIST TEXT TRANSLATION SOCIETY

Chairperson: The Venerable Master Hua
Abbot of Gold Mountain Dhyana Monastery
Professor of the Tripitaka and the Dhyanas

PRIMARY TRANSLATION COMMITTEE:
Chairpersons: Bhikshuni Heng Yin, Lecturer in Buddhism
Bhikshuni Heng Ch'ih, Lecturer in Buddhism

Members: Bhikshu Wei Sung, Lecturer in Buddhism
Bhikshu Heng Kuan, Lecturer in Buddhism
Bhikshu Heng Pai, Lecturer in Buddhism
Bhikshu Heng Yo, Lecturer in Buddhism
Bhikshu Heng Sure, Lecturer in Buddhism
Bhikshuni Heng Hsien, Lecturer in Buddhism
Bhikshuni Heng Chen, Lecturer in Buddhism
Bhikshuni Heng Ch'ing, Lecturer in Buddhism

Upasaka Huang Kuo-jen, Kung Fu Master, B.A.
Upasaka I Kuo-jung, Ph.D., UC Berkeley
Upasaka Kuo Yu Linebarger, M.A., San Francisco State Univ.
Upasika Kuo Chin Vickers

REVISION COMMITTEE:
Chairpersons: Bhikshu Heng Yo, Upasaka I Kuo-jung

Members: Bhikshu Heng Kuan
Bhikshu Heng Sure
Bhikshuni Heng Yin
Bhikshuni Heng Ch'ih
Bhikshuni Heng Hsien
Bhikshuni Heng Chen
Professor L. Lancaster, UC Berkeley
Professor M. Tseng, San Francisco State University
Upasaka Hsieh Ping-ying, author, professor, editor
Upasika Phoung Kuo-wu   Upasika I Kuo-han, B.A.
Upasaka Lee Kuo-ch'ien, B.A.
Upasaka Li Kuo-wei, M.A.   Upasika Kuo-chin Vickers
Upasaka Kuo Yu Linebarger

EIGHT REGULATIONS FOR BUDDHIST TEXT TRANSLATION
SOCIETY TRANSLATORS:

The translation of the Buddhist Tripitaka is work of such
magnitude that it could never be entrusted to a single person
working on his own. Above all, translations of Sutras must be
certified as the authentic transmission of the Buddha's proper
Dharma. Translations done under the auspices of the Buddhist
Text Translation Society, a body of more than thirty Sangha
members and scholars, bear such authority. The following eight
regulations govern the conduct of Buddhist Text Translation
Society translators:

1. A translator must free himself from motives of personal gain and reputation.

2. A translator must cultivate an attitude free from arrogance and conceit.

3. A translator must refrain from advertising himself and denigrating others.

4. A translator must not establish himself as the standard of correctness and supress the work of others with his fault-finding.

5. A translator must take the Buddha-mind as his own mind.

6. A translator must use the wisdom of the selective Dharma-eye to determine true principles.

7. A translator must request the Virtuous Elders from the ten directions to certify his translations.

8. A translator must endeavor to propagate the teachings by printing Sutras, Shastras, and Vinaya texts when his translations have been certified.

ALSO FROM THE BUDDHIST TEXT TRANSLATION SOCIETY

The Dharani Sutra with Commentary by the Venerable Master Hua. "This is an extraordinary book of a kind rarely found in English translation...Presented with the lively commentary of Tripitaka Master Hua...it belongs to a category of Buddhist works normally held to be secret and transmitted only from Master to disciple.

"Skeptics and philosophers who disdain what strikes them as magical practice would be well-advised to give this book a miss, whereas those who deem that Western civilization is the poorer for having abandoned magic in favor of treating the universe like a piece of clockwork, as Newton did, may find it intriguing; and those who quite seriously desire to gain a Bodhisattva-like Bodhi-Mind, or 'Heart of Great Compassion' may be encouraged to try putting the dharani to actual mantric use.

"Known in Chinese as the Ta-pei Chou, this dharani is recited over and over every day by tens of thousands of Chinese, Japanese, and other Far Eastern Buddhists. Indeed, it would be surprising to come upon a really serious Buddhist in that part of the world who did not know it by heart...As to the Sutra containing it, Master Hua informs us that very few Chinese have even heard of it and that those who have understood its meaning and are capable of explaining its principles are even fewer.

"I cannot conscientiously recommend this book to everybody, nor was it ever intended to be 'everyone's cup of tea'; but, if you... desire to become a compassionate Bodhisattva--as every Mahayana Buddhist does--then buy it!"

John Blofeld, author of The Wheel of Life, in Shambala Review of Books and Ideas, September, 1976.

Paperbound. With over 100 reprints of Secret School Woodblocks. 339 pp. $10.00.